MAKING THE MEDIA CONNECTION

Topic
Timing
Type of Media

The T-Connector Formula for Marketing and
Public Relations

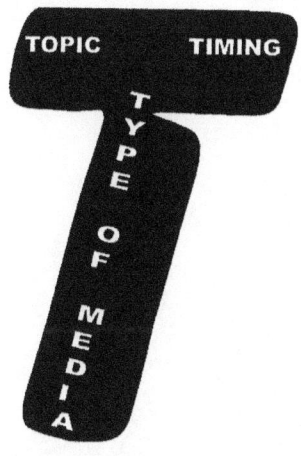

By Patricia Faulhaber

authorHOUSE®

AuthorHouse™
1663 Liberty Drive, Suite 200
Bloomington, IN 47403
www.authorhouse.com
Phone: 1-800-839-8640

First published by AuthorHouse 3/6/2009

ISBN: 978-1-4389-2504-2 (sc)

Library of Congress Control Number: 2009900897

Printed in the United States of America
Bloomington, Indiana

This book is printed on acid-free paper.

Contents

CHAPTER ONE
T-Connector Formula For Marketing And Public Relations   1

CHAPTER TWO
Marketing   13

CHAPTER THREE
Public Relations   21

CHAPTER FOUR
An Integrated Communications Plan   31

CHAPTER FIVE
Topic: The Message!   35

CHAPTER SIX
Know The Audience When Developing The Topic   51

CHAPTER SEVEN
Meet The Sample Companies   59

CHAPTER EIGHT
Topic And The Sample Companies   67

CHAPTER NINE
Timing   77

CHAPTER TEN
Audience And Timing   87

CHAPTER ELEVEN
Timing And The Sample Companies   91

CHAPTER TWELVE
Type Of Media   95

CHAPTER THIRTEEN
More About The Internet Media   107

CHAPTER FOURTEEN
More About Broadcast Media   113

CHAPTER FIFTEEN
Your Audience's Choice Of Media   117

CHAPTER SIXTEEN
Type Of Media And The Sample Companies   123

CHAPTER SEVENTEEN
So Let's Make The Connection   129

CHAPTER EIGHTEEN
Making The Connection With The Sample Companies   137

CHAPTER NINETEEN
Keeping The Connection   143

CHAPTER TWENTY
Crossing The T-connection   149

CHAPTER TWENTY-ONE
Keeping T-connected To Your Audience   155

APPENDIX A   159

APPENDIX B   161

APPENDIX C   164

CHAPTER ONE
INTRODUCTION
T-CONNECTOR FORMULA FOR MARKETING AND PUBLIC RELATIONS
Topic, Timing, and Type of Media

"There are no gains without pains."
Benjamin Franklin

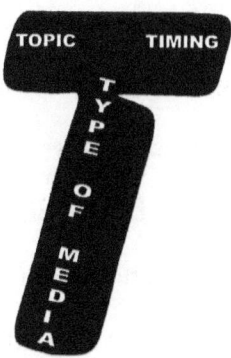

Business, industry, social service, government, education, large and small, and everyone in between use some form of communications, be it in sales, marketing, or public relations. Zig Ziglar wrote in his book, *Secrets of Closing the Sale*, that anyone who uses effective persuasion is, in effect, in the business of sales, no matter whom you are or where you work.

To be effective in today's world of commerce, everyone must also be in the business of communications. There is a saying that grows ever more important in the current competitive business world: "Out of sight, out of mind, out of business."

To be seen or heard, you need to have an edge, or a plan,

or a formula. The T-Connector Formula can help you successfully communicate with your company's or organization's publics.

WHAT IS THE T-CONNECTOR FORMULA?

There are three parts to the T-Connector Formula. Each part addresses one of the following issues:

1) Having the right topic or message

2) At the right time (and before deadline)

3) Communicating the message using the right type of media

The T-Connector Formula shows a business owner, manager, department head, nonprofit organization director, or public relations or marketing professional how to get the right message to the right type of media in the proper time frame. Put these three elements together, as illustrated below, they make a T-connection.

Topic Timing

T
y
p
e
o
f
m
e
d
i
a

WHY USE THE T-CONNECTOR FORMULA?

Face it, everyone communicating with marketing and public relations through the media is competing against each other for the same media time and space. Only a certain percentage will actually win the time and space they seek. Using a systematic, organized attempt with the T-Connector Formula can help put a company in the lead. Keep in mind the only way to guarantee print space or airtime is to buy it, as in paid advertising.

Professionally, I have over twenty years of experience in writing, public relations, sales, and marketing. I also have spent several years in sales management and have extensive experience in teaching and promoting adult education. I am also an avid reader. I have read hundreds of business-related books, including books on public relations and marketing.

What this book does is introduce you to the T-Connector Formula and shows you step-by-step how to use the formula effectively. The T-Connector Formula is a formula that first-time and long-time professionals can apply to the process of obtaining press time and space for their company or organization.

The main objectives of public relations and marketing are to promote, promote, and promote. You can do this by informing and persuading or buying advertising. No matter the medium, the T-Connector Formula provides an effective framework to get started on promoting, promoting, promoting.

MARKETING AND PUBLIC RELATIONS PROFESSIONALS

What kind of professional background or training and education do the best public relations and marketing professionals have to make them most effective in promoting, promoting, and promoting? Many start out going to college as journalism majors. Others start with marketing or communications majors or training.

The ultimate public relations professional knows their way around both the journalism and marketing or promotion worlds.

Journalists oftentimes change careers and enter the public relations arena. Having an ex-journalist in a public relations department can certainly help get the company's news in to print. On the downside, journalists are not trained to market or promote.

Professionally trained marketers, on the other hand, often lack the experience or knowledge of how to get company news to the public, but they know how to interpret demographics and they know about focus groups and product, place, and price.

It can be a difficult task to find the professional that has both backgrounds. You more than likely will have a marketing person and a public relations person or separate departments.

If your company does have two separate departments, to achieve maximum promotion, try combining or integrating the marketing and public relations departments into one powerful promotional machine.

This works so well because of the similarities of the activities for marketing and public relations. Both require the following:

- Planning
- Preparing
- Evaluating
- Implementing
- Communicating effectively

This book examines the communications link and how to best utilize topic, timing, and type of media (the T-Connector Formula) to effectively promote (market) and inform, persuade, and build solid relationships (public relations).

In other words, whether you work in public relations or marketing, or you are wearing many hats that include public relations and marketing, this book will benefit your publicity and promotional efforts.

USING THE T-CONNECTOR FORMULA TO WRITE YOUR COMMUNICATIONS

A company can have the best-written and well-intended mission rendered virtually useless if the company's publics never hear it or read it. Once again, keep in the mind the saying, "Out of sight, out of mind, out of business." A company must communicate to internal publics such as employees, stockholders, and suppliers. It must also stay in the minds of the external publics such as customers, clients, social agencies, community leaders, and the general public.

Your company's news and information is put in the external public's eye through marketing and public relations activities, which are carefully and thoroughly described in marketing and public relations plans (MRPR). News is distributed to the internal publics through public relations or via a well-planned communication effort from the administration. The T-Connector Formula helps to implement the communications sections of marketing and public relations plans.

There are in-depth theories to both marketing and public relations, so much so that there are college degrees in both disciplines. This book only takes a surface view of each. Chapter Two will define marketing as it relates to using the T-Connector Formula, and Chapter Three will explore the basics of public relations.

SIMILAR TASKS WITH A T-CONNECTOR IN THE MIDDLE

As stated earlier, marketing and public relations are usually separate processes but they do share similar tasks, and both depend on strategic planning.

This book takes just one part of each of these processes and explores it in depth. Knowing how to get your organization's "news" published for free is an important task in the public relations process, the results of which will automatically flow into the marketing process.

You must catch the attention of your target market (which by the way gets defined in the marketing and public relations planning phase), and this attention will generally result in increased customer traffic, which then becomes part of your marketing plan.

This book does not attempt to address marketing and public relations planning and implementation. It does try to help you develop and deliver the appropriate message at the appropriate time using the most effective type of media.

A COMBINED BUSINESS MODEL

A business model that combines the marketing and public relations functions into one big integrated marketing and public relations plan was developed in the 1990s but is still applicable today.

You may notice a few Ts in integrated marketing and public relations plan. The T-Connectors profiled throughout this book are important to the success of this business model. Just as the name implies, the marketing and public relations plans are combined into one model or plan. Chapter Four explains the basis for the model and illustrates a development chart.

PRESS RELEASES…A PUBLIC RELATIONS MAINSTAY

Press releases are the traditional means of informing the public of your company's news. They are one of the most effective tools in a public relations kit. Press releases can be far reaching in their effects.

Editors and reporters can and do pick up on feature stories and coverage from press releases. Releases do get read. Releases can get attention. And, press releases have gotten more versatile by having a Web site presence and a targeted audience persona.

While press releases have gotten more versatile, the same rules apply when creating: know the goal of the release, know the audience you want to read the release, write the release to that audience, and distribute the release accordingly to get the most effect. The T-Connector Formula can help.

ONE PART OR ONE T-CONNECTOR AT A TIME

Keep in mind, the T-Connectors to markeTing and public relaTions address just one part of the two processes. I have written that statement a number of times to make sure that you are aware of the planning that **must go** into marketing and public relations so that these two functions can produce the results for which their independent formulas were developed.

Another important item to keep in mind as you read through the book is that your company or organization must have the service or products and planning in place to substantiate the attention your company will most certainly generate with marketing and public relations. If not, the attention of your target market (or any market, for that matter) will hurt you instead of benefit. In other words, be prepared to deliver on all claims and be true to your words!

HOW IT ALL CONNECTS: STARTING WITH THE TOPIC

In her book *Communication Counts*, media and presentation

consultant, Mary Civiello writes about helping a client write a headline for a presentation. Civiello suggested the client think about the audience and what would excite them. The headline the two of them came up with was "Good PR Results in News You Can Use to Win New Clients". The presentation was for a group of magazine ad salespersons wanting to learn how to sell more ads for a magazine.

That is exactly what a public relations professional wants to develop when thinking of a topic – news you can use.

The Publicity Handbook by David R. Yale details that "Journalists want two things from publicists: your facts have to be reliable, and your material must have a news angle or news peg that makes it different and interesting."

This formula applies to proposing feature press coverage as well as sending press releases and public service announcements (PSAs). Chapter Five will give you detailed information on selecting a topic that fits the time. For a quick example or two, almost every month of the year has a special theme. November is American Diabetes Month. October is Adult Literacy Month in Ohio. January always has the New Year theme. May/June can always produce a "gear up for summer" note.

For standard press releases and PSAs, find or fit your message to what's relevant in local, state, or national news and events. Try a back-to-school fit and you'll be surprised at all the ways you can tie your message to this event, which by the way, happens all over the United States in late

August, early September.

As a public relations specialist for adult literacy, I always sent press releases in August informing the general public that registration for fall GED classes was happening. Registration and classes were held year round, but since everyone's thinking of returning to school in the fall or at the beginning of a new year, I sent registration releases in August and again in January for spring registration.

I sent the same set of releases in May and geared the message to spend your summer preparing for your GED or enhancing your reading, math, or English skills in preparation for fall college courses.

For feature stories or press coverage, you can tie the topic to what's happening in the "big" news of the time, the season, or what's happening in the area. We had an adult literacy class take a class trip to the county Board of Elections. On the surface it doesn't seem newsworthy, except that it was before the 2000 presidential election and many in the class had never voted. The adult students were unsure of how to use the voting booths or what happened to their votes.

Visiting the Board of Elections helped the students feel more comfortable, and most returned on Election Day to vote. One of the local newspapers decided to cover the story because of those who had never voted before but wanted to. And, what a presidential election it turned out to be!

Think about those involved with an event. Are they involved with community organizations? Do they have outside interests in nonprofits, social service agencies, or public service?

How about the event itself? Is your company installing new equipment that will increase production or quality? Will your company's event increase employment in the community? Is the equipment being installed the latest and greatest technology in the area, in the state, or in the country?

In the public relations chapter you'll learn that the main purpose of public relations activities is to inform and persuade your organization's publics of what is going on in your company. There are a number of questions you can ask yourself about the topic that will help you prepare your message, place it with perfect timing, and reach your audience in the appropriate manner with the perfect type of media.

No matter the news or message, you'll need to determine who needs to hear it, what they need to know, why they need to know, and where or how they will hear the information. Chapter Six will give you more help with determining the answers.

TIMING IS EVERYTHING

We've already touched on timing a bit and it will be further explored in Chapter Nine. For now, realize that timing refers to making the information relevant to the time of the year. It also refers to getting the information to the selected media before deadline. Chapter Ten discusses the issues of audience and timing.

TYPE OF MEDIA

You need to build and maintain a media list. You know the message you want to deliver, who it should go to, and when your deadline(s) is. Next you need to find the type of media that will best deliver the news. Just for the record, you may need to modify the message to fit the media.

Chapter Twelve will give complete details on how to find the media in your area, how to build and maintain a media list, and how to write and develop topics to the media type. Chapters Thirteen and Fourteen explore media outlets, while Chapter Fifteen looks at your audience's selection of media types. Again, there will be a series of questions that you can answer to help you complete this connection.

MAKING THE CONNECTION

After you learn some background information about marketing and public relations and after an in-depth look at preparing the communications plan of marketing and public relations with the appropriate topic, timing, and type of media, Chapter Seventeen will help you make the connection. Chapters Nineteen and Twenty provide more tips and information on maintaining connections. Chapters Seven, Eight, Eleven, Sixteen, and Eighteen show you how two sample companies use the T-Connector Formula to effectively plan promoting, promoting, and promoting.

CHAPTER TWO

MARKETING

"He that waits upon fortune is never sure of a dinner."
Benjamin Franklin

Although this book is not a marketing book, an understanding of marketing is needed. After learning about marketing, we'll zoom in on the communications aspects of marketing, which is the area where the T-Connector Formula works.

TELL ME ABOUT MARKETING

I thought you'd never ask. One of the hundreds of technical definitions of marketing goes something like this: Marketing is a social and managerial process involving fulfilling the needs and wants of groups of individuals. It involves creating and exchanging products, services, and value.

A less technical definition might be that marketing is a wide range of functions or activities that help your company meet the needs of your customers or clients. Simply, marketing is the act of selling products or services in a defined market. The market is defined by the wants and needs of customers or clients your company intends to service.

For example, if you market adult technical education, you're fulfilling an educational need for adults. Your market then becomes those adults in need of technical education. Those adults seeking a four-year college degree are not in your primary market.

In January of 2008, www.marketingpower.com published a press release from the American Marketing Association detailing their new definition of marketing:

"Marketing is the activity, set of institutions and processes for creating, communicating, delivering, and exchanging offerings that have value for customers, clients, partners, and society at large."

Marketing, in comparison to public relations, is more "ad"-ventorial in nature as opposed to editorial, which is what public relations tends to produce.

When you have your market defined and your product or service developed, the next step is to develop a marketing plan.

THE MARKETING PLAN

Simply and directly stated, a marketing plan is a written agenda defining an organization's objectives. It also outlines the marketing steps needed to realize those objectives. The marketing plan identifies customers, product development, company image, sales and advertising objectives, and for some companies, public relations activities.

To be effective, the plan:

+ Must be written—it must be written—it must be written

+ Must be based on research

+ Should include the basic four components of the marketing mix: product, price, promotion, and place. It is imperative to your company's survival to have a marketing plan. Following are several diagrams that illustrate the marketing objectives (Diagram 2-1), what's included in the marketing plan (Diagram 2-2), and the integrated yet separate parts of communications based marketing (Diagram 2-3).

MARKETING OBJECTIVES
Diagram 2-1

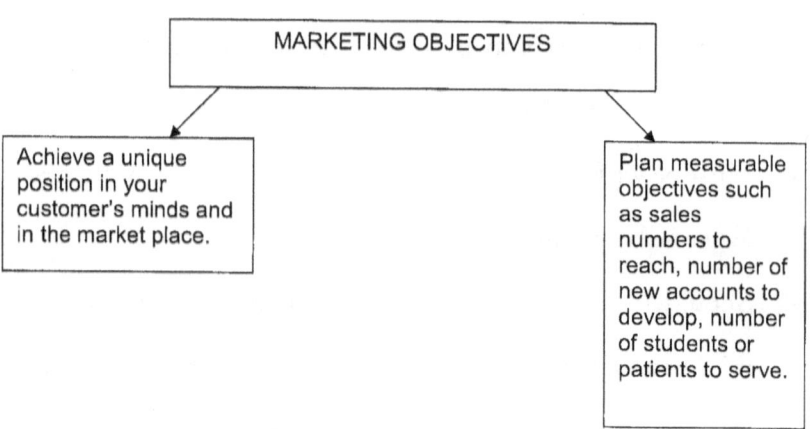

MARKETING OBJECTIVES

Achieve a unique position in your customer's minds and in the market place.

Plan measurable objectives such as sales numbers to reach, number of new accounts to develop, number of students or patients to serve.

MARKETING PLAN
Diagram 2-2

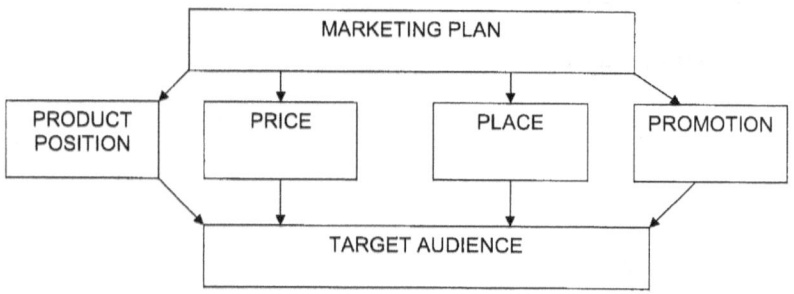

MARKETING PLAN

PRODUCT POSITION

PRICE

PLACE

PROMOTION

TARGET AUDIENCE

Communications in Marketing
Diagram 2-3

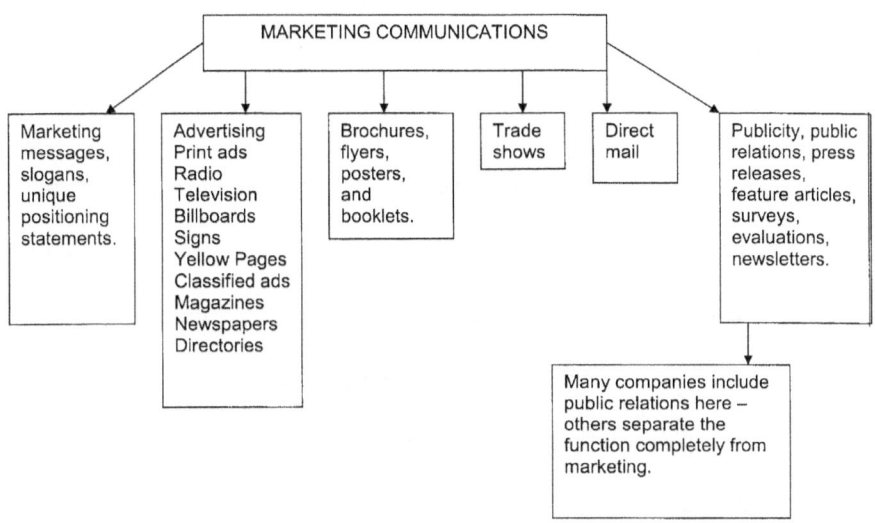

MARKETING COMMUNICATIONS

| Marketing messages, slogans, unique positioning statements. | Advertising Print ads Radio Television Billboards Signs Yellow Pages Classified ads Magazines Newspapers Directories | Brochures, flyers, posters, and booklets. | Trade shows | Direct mail | Publicity, public relations, press releases, feature articles, surveys, evaluations, newsletters. |

Many companies include public relations here – others separate the function completely from marketing.

According to the book, *Streetwise Marketing Plan* by Don Debelak, you can find numerous definitions of marketing, but in its simplest meaning, it boils down to meeting the following goals:

1. Give the customer what they want.

2. Your company differentiates itself from the competition with features, service, price, or distribution.

3. Deliver high impact marketing messages through advertising, brochures, booklets, and other channels listed in Diagram 2-3.

4. Develop unique positioning statements or descriptive statements that marketing and public relations use to set a company, organization, or product apart from the competition.

5. Place the product or service in distribution so that the customer can easily purchase it.

6. Provide continued support and customer service.

There are many proven formulas and explanations for marketing, and I've read, studied, and used many of them. When you meet the six goals listed above, you are developing and implementing an effective marketing plan

These goals need to be reviewed every year with appropriate changes made to the company's strategic planning, which should always include marketing and public relations.

MAKING THE T-CONNECTION

The T-Connector Formula works anywhere in the marketing process that requires effective communications. Examples include paid advertising, brochures, letters, posters, business cards, Web sites, or any category that uses written, verbal, or visuals to communicate or connect with a market. The effects of good public relations are critical to the marketing function.

Good public relations and good press have helped to build companies like amazon.com and ebay.com. Good press has built successful brands like Cabbage Patch Kids, the Ford Mustang, Barbie, Tylenol, and Viagra. Look at all the good press books on the best-sellers list get, like the Harry Potter series, *Who Moved My Cheese*, and the Dummy computer books, all of which used undeniable good topic, timing, and type of media to meet their marketing and communications goals.

If your company can reach the press, your company's marketing plan will soar. Think of the T-Connector as the talking or telling part of marketing. One of the most effective vehicles to deliver the telling part is through the media.

MORE TO SAY THAN WE HAVE ROOM FOR

There is so much more to say about marketing; unfortunately, there is not space enough in this book. Our concern with marketing at this point is to get the communications functions into the publics' eye or into their ear, which involves fitting the topic to the time and getting it produced in the right type of media.

Suffice it to say that marketing leads the way for advertising, sales, and public relations. All use some form of communications directed to the publics your company or organization is involved with. An effective communications plan developed with the T-Connector Formula easily accommodates marketing and public relations.

The next two sections explore public relations and integrating all of the communications and promotional aspects of your organization. Beyond those two chapters, we delve into topic, timing, and type of media.

CHAPTER THREE

PUBLIC RELATIONS

"Now by press we can speak to nations. And good books and well-written pamphlets have great and general influence."
Benjamin Franklin

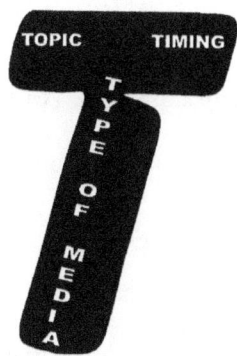

Learning the basics of public relations will help you use the T-Connector Formula effectively.

THE BASICS OF PUBLIC RELATIONS

Here we go again with the technical definitions. Public relations is also a management function that is a deliberate, planned two-way communication process involving informing and persuading the public in their own best interest.

There are many, many definitions of public relations. Here is one definition provided by www.managementhelp.org:

"Public relations includes ongoing activities to ensure the overall company has a strong public image. Public relations activities include helping the public to understand the company and its products. Often, public relations are conducted through the media, that is newspapers, television, magazines, etc. ...public relations is often considered as one of the primary activities included in promotions."

Many believe that public relations is about building strong relationships with a company's clients, customers, employee, stockholders, and all publics related to the company. And, that publicity or media attention is just one tool in the public relations toolbox.

Simply, public relations' primary purpose is to inform and persuade. You inform your audiences or populations about your company's service, product, position, free offers, news, etc.

As you inform the audience, you also persuade them that they can trust and believe in (and buy from) your company. One of the simplest definitions I've read about public relations is to think of it as "public relaytions," because with public relations you are relaying information to your publics.

Michael Levine in his book *Guerrilla P.R. 2.0* writes, "I define what I do as gift-wrapping. If you package a bracelet in a Tiffany Box, it will have a higher perceived value than if presented in a Kmart box."

Levine also wrote, "Likewise, on a more mundane scale, one will succeed in a P.R. campaign only if the perception fostered truly resonates with the public."

PLANNING FOR EFFECTIVE PUBLIC RELATIONS

Regardless of your personal definition of public relations, to succeed, public relations functions have to build around a well-designed and well-written plan—a public relations plan.

A public relations plan is a written agenda for presenting the image of the company or organization (which is usually defined in the marketing plan) and is based on public relations principles.

CHARTING THE PATH OF PUBLIC RELATIONS

In his book, *Value-Added Public Relations*, Thomas L. Harris states, "The ability of public relations to identify issues that impact marketing, to handle crisis situations, and to counsel top management, can exact enormous influence on marketing success or failure."

Public relations and marketing have become increasingly intertwined or integrated. With public relations, you inform the public in an effort to persuade them to use your company or products or support your organization by relating the value of doing so, which is best accomplished through the use of communications and the media. Al Ries and Laura Ries stated in their book, *The Fall of Advertising & The Rise of Public Relations*, that "advertising is a continuation of public relations by other means and should be started only after a public relations program has run its course."

Advertising is generally part of the marketing plan but it has communications at the center, so the T-Connector Formula can be applied to advertising as well as marketing and public relations.

The following flowchart shows how public relations, marketing, and advertising are linked. The second chart shows all the different communication channels or media types that are used in your company's communication efforts.

Integrating marketing and public relations (and advertising, for that matter) into one communications plan strengthens the overall effectiveness of all the individual processes.

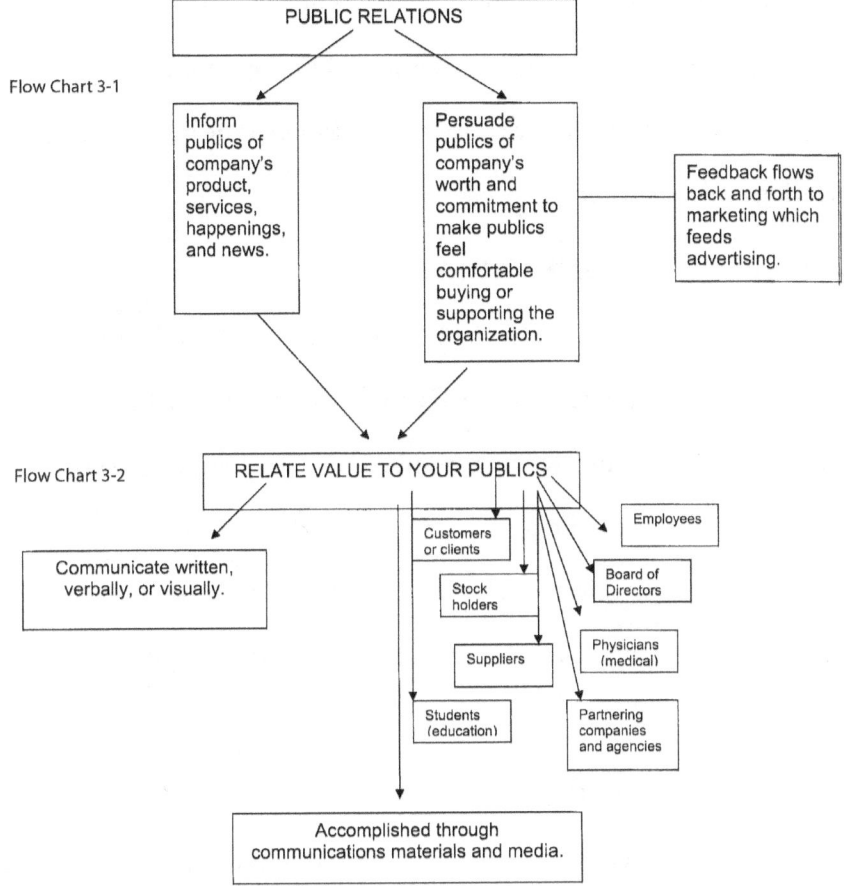

PUBLIC RELATIONS

Flow Chart 3-1

Inform publics of company's product, services, happenings, and news.

Persuade publics of company's worth and commitment to make publics feel comfortable buying or supporting the organization.

Feedback flows back and forth to marketing which feeds advertising.

Flow Chart 3-2

RELATE VALUE TO YOUR PUBLICS

Communicate written, verbally, or visually.

Customers or clients

Employees

Stock holders

Board of Directors

Suppliers

Physicians (medical)

Students (education)

Partnering companies and agencies

Accomplished through communications materials and media.

As you can see from the charts, public relations rely heavily on communications. There are a number of dimensions to public relations including planning, crisis management, implementation, evaluation, and measurement. Since the T-Connector Formula centers on topic, timing, and type of media to better ensure that the news of the company reaches the proper audiences at the right time and in the right form, we'll leave the definitions of the public relations functions to the many other public relations reference books.

PUBLIC RELATIONS VARIABLES

There are several variables from the public relations process that build into the T-Connector Formula that we do need to discuss, all having to do with effective communications. The following sections will explore the 5Ws and the 5Ps.

We will also look at another tried-and-true formula used in advertising, AIDA, that easily applies to public relations communications.

WHO, WHAT, WHERE, WHY, WHEN, HOW

The five Ws of journalism can be applied to news releases, advertising, and just about any type of communications a company can produce. Always double-check all communications to ensure the intended audience can easily tell who the message is directed at, what the message is, why the message is important, how and where to act upon the message. The Ws apply more strongly in the topic section of the T-Connector Formula, so they will be detailed in Chapter Five.

THE 5PS

As if the Ws weren't enough to remember, communications in

public relations has the obligation to relay to the audiences: 1) the point of the message, 2) the purpose of the message, 3) a perspective of the message that relates to each person in the target audience, 4) proof that what the message says is true, and 5) the people involved with the message. Again this section relies heavily in the topic part of the T-Connector Formula. As such, the 5Ps will be further explored in Chapter Five.

AIDA—AN ADVERTISING FORMULA THAT APPLIES TO PUBLIC RELATIONS

Another important acronym that applies to public relations happens to also be one of the oldest advertising formulas: AIDA. Get the Attention of the customer, create Interest for the customer to keep reading, develop Desire for the customer to want to know more, and then request the customer to take Action, such as calling you for more information.

Although this book does not address advertising directly, it has been referenced a number of times. Advertising is another one of those disciplines, like marketing or public relations, that deserves more space than this book affords. For the purpose of the T-Connector formula, advertising is mentioned because of its communications foundation and for how it is linked to public relations and marketing.

Take billboards, for example. Billboards are paid advertising and are developed through advertising professionals. Generally, billboards are used to relay a public relations message showing value, commitment, and building trust. To further link this example, billboard campaigns are part of the marketing plan.

Even billboards can use the T-Connectors. It has to be the right topic (message) for the right timing (geographies, seasonal, demographics, who drives the road, etc.) to fit this type of media. Billboards have to be a quick read with graphics that make an impression and are easily remembered.

MORE TO PR THAN FITS THIS CHAPTER

Public relations has always played a crucial role in the success of organizations, of personalities, in the political arena, and in government. This section defined what public relations does, and I only gave you a nutshell version. If you need a better understanding of public relations, there are many books and professional journals that you can read to get an overview of public relations.

INFORMING AND PERSUADING EFFECTIVELY USING THE T-CONNECTOR FORMULA

The T-Connector Formula helps you match the topic, timing, and the type of media to best inform and persuade your publics. Internal or external publics all get their news differently. One person's news is another person's blah-blah.

My twenty-nine-year-old son and his circle of friends seldom read the printed newspaper. Their daily news comes at the end of a mouse through a cursor shining through a computer monitor. And, it is available to them 24/7. His friends are less interested in politics and more interested in technology news.

If his group happened to be in your target audience, you would need to set your topics to get their attention in the media that will reach them at their preferred time of day. The T-Connector Formula will help you find the needed answers and direct your topic, timing, and type of media.

CAN WE COMBINE THE COMMUNICATIONS PLANS?

Glad you asked that question. The next section looks at using an integrated communications plan that accommodates the communication needs of marketing and public relations.

CHAPTER FOUR

AN INTEGRATED COMMUNICATIONS PLAN

*Benjamin Franklin published the first trade catalog in 1744
containing a list of books Franklin was offering for sale by mail.*

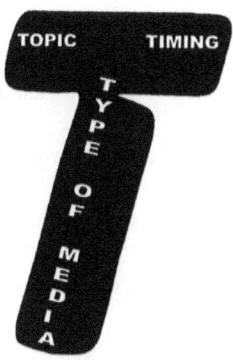

A quick recap is in order. We know that marketing in a nutshell is adventorial and concerns itself with defining markets and providing products and services to meet market needs. We also know how important the communication process is to marketing.

Then we learned that public relations is editorial in nature and is concerned with the tasks of getting your company's news to your company's publics, be they internal or external. We know of the enormous communications tasks required to get the public relations job done.

Next we need to explore the business model that combines marketing and public relations into one communications plan.

WHAT IS THE MRPR PLAN?

The marketing and public relations plan is one central plan that defines and combines marketing and public relations into one communications plan. Just as each of the individual plans already outlined in Chapters Two and Three, an MRPR plan must be:

+ Written

+ Based on current and up-to-date research

+ Inclusive of all aspects of marketing

+ Inclusive of all aspects of public relations

THE INTEGRATED MODEL CHARTED

Take a look at the chart below for an illustration of the integrated communications plan.

THE INTEGRATED COMMUNICATION MODULE
Diagram 4-1

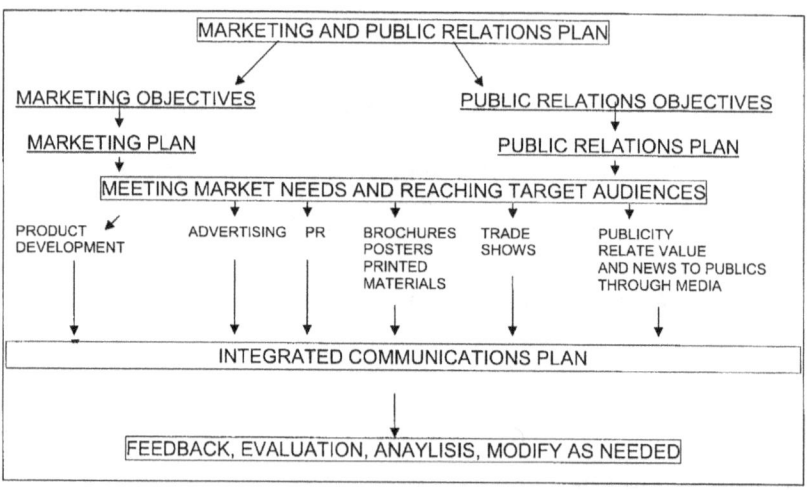

BOTTOM LINE

The bottom line in the MRPR integrated plan is that instead of marketing and public relations doing separate planning, the two functions plan together. Both functions rely on communications, media, and any other tools used to reach a company's publics so heavily that it makes perfect sense and a streamlined practice to combine the two. Using one communications plan will also ensure a consistent message.

Topic, timing, and type of media (the T-Connector Formula) apply throughout all of the materials on the chart that go into the communications plan. What is the message (topics) and when should the message be delivered (timing) to the targeted audiences? What is the best way to reach the target audiences (type of media)?

WE HAVE THE BASIS OF THE BUSINESS TERMS

With all the preliminaries of learning about marketing, public relations, and integrated communications, it is time to look in detail at the topic, timing, and type of media formula.

A WORD ABOUT FEEDBACK

A two-way communications process only works when you ask for and listen to your audiences. All of your marketing, public relations, and integrated communications plans must allow for ways to accommodate feedback. As you go through the remainder of this book, keep in mind that feedback can and should help you further define topic, timing, and type of media. Please your audiences by reaching them how, when, why, and where they want to be reached.

CHAPTER FIVE

TOPIC: THE MESSAGE!

*"Bring a hundred or thousand fold to him who
appreciates the advantages of the 'the printer's ink.'"*

One of P.T. Barnum's
Ten keys to business success

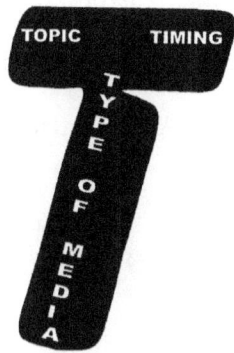

Topic. The message. Think it through. What do you want to say? To whom do you want to say it?

Find a topic that fits the time of the year; get it to the editor before the publication's deadline, and only send it to the type of media that fits the topic. This is the stuff the T-Connector Formula—topic, timing, and type of media—is made of.

How does an editor decide to print one story over another? When working in public relations, you'll read plenty of articles telling you that newspaper and magazine editors receive hundreds of press releases and news tips per day.

How will your press release ever make it to the top of the

selection list and into print, or make it onto the airwaves through radio or television broadcasts?

YOU CAN INCREASE YOUR CHANCES BY

There are several elements every news release or PSA must have. To get your press release at least noticed, you need to get the mechanics of the release or announcement in order. Formatting is one type of mechanic; having complete information is another. You need to build both into every release and PSA. Formatting is discussed later in this chapter. Most important to this book is developing the topic.

There are a number of ways to help you build the topic. The 5Ws, the 5Ps, different message strategies, finding the relevance, and putting a theme to the message are all part of building the topic.

REMEMBER THE 5WS AND THE 5PS?

Do you remember your teachers in school suggesting that you dot your i's and cross your t's before walking away from a test or an application? In writing public relations and marketing pieces, you do this by checking to see if you have included information about the who, what, where, when, and how: the 5Ws.

The *New York Times* prints all the news that's fit. Your news releases need to have all the news that fits the print space right at the top, and all the Ws and Ps have to be there. Each communications developed must have the who, what, where, when, and how provided in clear, simple, and straightforward language that fits the intended audience.

Got news about a free lecture you would like to have the local newspaper publicize? Be sure to include the name of the lecture, the cost of the lecture (even though it is free), where the lecture will be held, the time of the lecture, why the lecture is important, and how the reader can register or find out more information.

Actually write out directions such as: "Automated Sales Invoicing is a free lecture that will show accounting and bookkeeping personnel how to save up to two hours a day when completing sales invoice posting. To register, call 555-555-5555." (who, how, what , why) "The lecture will be held on May 1, 2009 at 3:00 p.m. in room 202 at the Technology School for Beginners." (where and when)

The 5Ps provide the <u>point</u> of the message, the <u>purpose</u> of the message, the <u>perspective</u> to the reader's life, and the <u>proof</u> that the company can and will deliver on what the message states; the 5Ps always involves <u>people</u>.

Building on the press release started above, to include the 5Ps, the release may continue as follows:

"Statistics for 2002 show that over 90percent of small businesses use automated accounting software to write checks for purchases and payroll. Only 10 percent use automatic sales invoice posting." (perspective) "XYZ Computer Company is hosting a free lecture" (the point of the release) "to help accountants and bookkeepers understand the time-saving features of sales invoicing." (purpose).

"The XYZ Computer Company has helped over 300 companies implement sales invoicing." (proof) "Mr. Dollar, chief accountant from ABC Sales states, 'My company went from taking three days to post sales invoices to three hours.'" (people and more proof)

Another important characteristic of the above release, as it should be with every release and media contact, is that only **one message** is conveyed. The free lecture is the news, everything else enhances or builds up the news of the free lecture.

Get in the habit of checking for the 5Ws and the 5Ps to ensure a complete message every time.

CUSTOMIZING YOUR PITCH

Before getting into the specifics of developing your topic, customizing the pitch needs to be discussed. Falling into the "one-size-fits-all, sure-to-be-rejected" trap is fatal to getting your news published.

Newspapers, magazines, radio, and television suffer economic times as hard as anyone else. That means fewer editors, fewer pages for news, and a harder time getting your releases into the news. Keep in mind as you read the remainder of this chapter that customizing the topic to fit the publication is a must. Your message needs to address the readers, listeners, or viewers of each type of media.

Your message needs to fit the style and purpose of the media outlet you will use. For example, the style and purpose of *Business Week* magazine is much different from the style and purpose of *Woman's Day* magazine. Those interested in the business environment read one magazine, while women interested in family or home environment read the other. You can reach out to both types of readers, but you need to change the style of your release to fit each desired market.

Think of it as emotion promotion. The writing style needs to fit the readers' style and emotion.

Your company's news can make it into local, state, regional, and national media if it is prepared to reach the different audiences in a relevant and meaningful manner. The only way to effectively customize your message or topic is to know the media you are trying to get your news into; we'll talk more about this later.

MESSAGE STRATEGIES

In his book, *Public Relations Writing—The Essentials of Style and Format,* Thomas H. Bivins defines two message strategies: informative and persuasive. This follows the definition of public relations: to inform and to persuade your publics. Let's take a closer look at the two strategies.

Informative messages are free from expression and are written in the narrative (story-telling) manner.

To inform an audience, consider:

+ Why does the audience need to know this information?

- What precisely do they need to know?

- Are the objectives of the message clear enough to measure the effectiveness?

- Does your message raise the level of knowledge of the target audience?

<u>Persuasive</u> messages are audience centered. The message is based on who the audience is and includes:

- Identification of who you are.

- A suggestion of action required by the audience.

- Familiarity and trust.

- The message is clear and simple.

LET'S CHART THE CHARACTERISTICS

Diagram 5-1 provides a quick view of the characteristics of informative and persuasive message strategies.

INFORMATIVE AND PERSUASIVE CHARACTERISTICS
Diagram 5-1

Informative	Persuasive
Message is balanced and complete. Let readers in on something. Use to introduce a new product or service or use when you need to set the record straight. Write just the facts.	Heavy on the positive attributes of the product, service or viewpoint. Use words that invoke emotion (emotion promotion). Include a call to action.

Informative and Persuade

Message is balanced and complete.

Let readers in on something.

Heavy on the positive attributes of the product, service or viewpoint.

Use to introduce a new product or service or use when you need to set the record straight.

Write just the facts.

Includes a call to action.

FIT THE MESSAGE TO THE AUDIENCE

Prepare your press release or PSA with all the 5Ws and 5Ps. Setting the pace by informing, persuading, or both opens the way for you to determine the audience and start directing the topic. When determining the audience, keep in mind the types of audiences you may be addressing such as:

+ A hostile audience that may never be convinced.

+ A sympathetic audience that really doesn't need to be convinced.

+ An undecided audience that can be convinced by your competitor as well as by you. A rational message is needed for this group.

+ A friendly audience that needs to read an emotional appeal (emotion promotion).

+ A neutral or disinterested audience that needs an attention-getter message.

+ An uninformed audience that needs to be informed.

In conjunction with determining these general definitions of your audience, you need to define the demographics of your audience. Are they male or female? Is the audience young, old, or in between? How much money do they make? Are they decision-makers?

To catch the attention of Caucasian males between the ages of twenty-five and forty-four, I might start my release with startling statistics aimed right at them. The beginning of the release would go something like: "In the past two years, over 35percent of white males between the ages of 25-44 have gotten service-related technology jobs."

Upcoming chapters will help you with writing to your audience.

FIND THE RELEVANCE

Make your release relevant to the hard news happening in your area. Are area churches collecting food and clothing over the holidays? Did your company collect an inordinate amount of items for donations? If so, you've got the basis for a great press release. Write it up and send it off.

Did your company develop a new product that saves on fuel or energy? If so, you now have great press potential. There are many issues at large these days. Unemployment, interest rates, rising consumer prices, crime, and pollution are just a few of the pertinent topics of today. Read local newspapers and company trade magazines or watch the evening news and you'll find many ways your company is contributing to making things better.

By some estimates, the average consumer is exposed to about 3,000 marketing messages a day; this number is quickly increasing with all of the online advertising going on these days. To prevent your news from being just another piece of information on the junk pile, make it relevant to the reader. Make your press benefit the reader instead of wasting their time.

THEME IT BUT BE CONSISTENT

You can also write your press release around a theme. Look at how many times the phrase "Give yourself the gift of education" is used in advertising college or adult education courses.

Back to school happens every fall and makes a great theme to build your news around. One word of warning here: Be careful, when applying a theme, that you don't lose your message.

For instance, if you use a back-to-school theme, don't let the theme overpower the message. For example, if you are XYZ Backpack Inc., your back-to-school press release could go something like this:

"Back to school means backpacking it for the next nine months to your children. XYZ Backpack Inc., producers of Health Smart Backpacks, offers a free list of backpack health and safety tips.

"Improperly sized backpacks can mean back problems, stooped shoulders, or stressed neck muscles for your children. Call 1-555-555-5555 to receive your free list of backpack tips."

The theme of back to school is stated up front but is replaced by the message of how XYZ can help your children's return to school be more healthy.

TOPIC QUESTIONS: REMEMBER, INFORM, PERSUADE, OR INFORM AND PERSUADE

Get in the habit of asking yourself the following questions when determining a topic:

1. Who is the audience for this message?
2. What does this audience need to know?

3. Why does the audience need to know?

4. When does the audience need to know?

5. Where is the audience most likely to hear the message?

6. What is the uniqueness you give this topic?

7. How can you link the topic to current events?

FINDING NEWSWORTHY FACTS IN YOUR ORGANIZATION

Whether you are writing a news release or PSA or promoting a press conference or special event, find the newsworthiness in every media submission. Then, add a special twist by the finding the excitement in the story. The following questions can get you started:

1. Is the information hard news, breaking news, or human interest (does it have a soft side to it)?

2. What type of journalist would want to see the information?

3. Does the information answer the 5Ws and the 5Ps?

4. How is the product, service, event, or person exciting or different from others in the same type of business?

5. What does it do for the readers, listeners, etc.? For example, does it save time or money, improve one's health, or teach a new skill?

6. What is the human story behind the product, service, event, or person?

7. Can you find interesting statistics or research to report?

8. Can you get a quote to include from someone associated with your company that expresses a compelling opinion or statement?

DEVELOPING A NEWSWORTHY ANGLE

The news angle can determine whether an editor takes an interest in your release. You can take the same set of facts and develop numerous angles. What makes you the public relations or communications professional that you are is how you select the angle that will interest the media (and ultimately their readers, listeners, or surfers).

The T-Connector Formula can help you answer the following questions:

1. What are the facts and benefits of your news release?
2. Do those facts and benefits present a news angle or peg that is seasonal, possibly a world record, or creating a debate or controversy?
3. Does your news link with any local people, experts, or events?
4. Can your local story get any national media coverage?

That's a lot to remember about developing your topic. As you work with your organization's events and happenings, you'll get to where you can see and write the topic in your mind and have all the pieces in place by the time you commit it to digital form or paper.

FINDING THE LOCAL ANGLES

As with developing a big news angle, you can also look at local news and area happenings to link your topic. The following questions may help you to do just that:

1. Can you add local statistics to news item?

2. Can you refer to or quote local experts?

3. Can you attribute the news item to several local experts, spokespersons, government officials, or supporters?

4. Is the news item revolutionary, new to the area, the latest in technology, or a new service your company has brought to the area?

A WORD ABOUT THE MECHANICS

As promised, this section discusses, very briefly, the hard skills of writing press releases and public service announcements. With so many press releases and news items crossing an editor's desk, they only have time to consider properly prepared releases. No matter the angle or how your topic is related to the big news, if you fax a handwritten release that is three pages in length, forget about seeing it the local newspaper, because your piece is going in the trashcan.

Use the list below as a checklist when you first start preparing releases. After a while—and if you are using a computer and word processing program—really, who isn't?—you'll be able to keep a formatted copy and only change the content. Practice makes perfect, and you will be preparing many releases from this point on; you'll just automatically follow these formatting musts:

1. Press releases must be written in the third person.

2. All releases should be limited to one page (two pages at the absolute most).

3. Always double-space your releases.

4. Always send releases on official company letterhead.

5. Include contact information such as name and phone number in the first part of the release, usually in the upper right-hand corner (but it can be anywhere in the top section).

6. Always put the release date in the upper right-hand corner after the contact name and phone number.

7. Separate multiple pages with "(more)" at the bottom of each page. At the top of each additional page include "Release Name—Add 1." At the end of the release, put one of the following: ###, ---30---, or (30). The ### or 30 indicates the end of the release.

8. When emailing releases, put your logo at the top of the word processing document, then convert the document to a PDF file before sending electronically to an editor.

9. Always write public service announcements in the first person, in script format, double-spaced, and all on one page.

10. For editorials and letters to the editor, you should check the format required by calling the newspaper or magazine (or find the information inside the publication itself).

ADDITIONAL FORMATTING TIPS FOR WRITING NEWS RELEASES

When writing your news or press releases, always include the most important information at the very top of the release. Editors use a pattern called the "inverted pyramid" so that they can easily cut parts of the story to fit the space they have available. Because of this, you'll want to put the meat of the release at the top.

This pattern also saves the editor precious time in reading the release. The big news is at the top and should quickly catch the editor's attention. The release starts with the *lead*, then goes onto the *bridge*, used to bridge from the lead to the *body*, which provides information to support the lead. Finally, at the end, make the offer to find out more information by calling your company's telephone number (also referred to as the *call to action*).

Enough about the mechanics; let's get back to the T-Connector Formula.

GET READY TO MEET THE SAMPLE COMPANIES

Chapter Seven will introduce two fictional companies that we will follow as they use the T-Connector Formula. The first company is the Tree Top Company, a retail nursery and garden supply company.

The second sample company is Community Educational Services, a grant-funded not-for-profit organization that helps adults find college, technical schools, and training and funding or financing for tuition.

Both companies use marketing, public relations, paid advertising, press releases, and PSAs, and they appear regularly on local cable television shows. Generally, local cable television shows are reserved for nonprofit organizations; although Tree Top is a for-profit, the company does numerous community-related events, which allows them to use local cable television programming.

CHAPTER SIX

KNOW THE AUDIENCE WHEN DEVELOPING THE TOPIC

"Few corporations have enjoyed such a privileged relationship with their customers. It is part of the 'eBay phenomenon.'"
David Burrell
The eBay Phenomenon

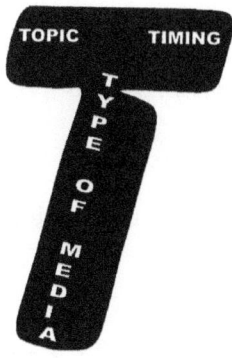

Remember: Always know thy audience. I've mentioned this in previous sections. You have no doubt read this statement elsewhere and possibly even had a course or two on what it means to know your audience.

It's so simple. It's so straightforward. It's soooo important. And, it is so often forgotten. I've had people ask me if their company would benefit from a profile or feature on local news and talk shows, or should they just publish their news releases on their Web site.

I always ask in return whether their clients or customers watch the local news and talk shows, or do they use the Internet as a consumer or news source. If they say that their customers read the local daily newspaper for information, then my reply is that they belong in the local newspaper.

Getting on the local news or a talk show will get the company exposure and expand their public relations efforts. But, unless the consumer listening is in need of your company's services or products, the efforts will be a fleeting attempt to build yourself as a quality company in the mind of that particular consumer.

The general consumer may be impressed with your company's profile, but they will forget you, your company, and your product or service by the time they turn off the television unless they need you and are part of your target audience.

START WITH RESEARCH FROM THE PR OR BUSINESS PLAN

If you are not sure who your target audience is, you can learn much of what you need to know about your audience in your company's marketing and public relations plan or business plan. If your company does not have a marketing and public relations plan, you'll want to develop and implement one as soon as you can.

You can learn the following about your audience from the marketing and public relations plan:

- + Who is the defined target audience?
- + Who uses your company's services or products?
- + Who recommends your company's services or products?

- Where is your audience located?

- Who are the decision-makers?

- How are referrals generated?

- What information is important to the decision-makers?

- What media outlets are used by your audiences?

You can make good media connections and apply the T-Connector Formula if you can also learn the following from the marketing and public relations plan:

- What are your company's long-term goals?

- What messages or themes were referenced in the business plan?

- What ideas, concepts, or themes were identified in the plan as being acceptable by your target audiences?

- What differentiates your company from the competition?

- What is your company's position in the marketplace (top provider, number two in the industry, up and coming, on the decline)?

People in your company put a lot of thought and time in developing business plans and marketing and public relations plans. Unfortunately, when these plans are completed, many in the company or organization forget about what is contained in the plans and operate in a manner they feel is appropriate. Take the time to get to know your company or organization by studying and referencing these plans as often as you can—it will pay off in the messages.

OTHER WAYS TO GET TO KNOW YOUR AUDIENCE

If you do not have access to a business plan or marketing and public relations plan, you can still define your company's target audiences. One of the easiest ways to define your audience is to list all of the possible people your communications have to reach at one time or another, for one reason or another. The list can help you know and understand the people you need to reach. To get you started, your audiences (you will always have more than one audience) might include the following:

Banks/creditors
Board of directors
Business-to-business
Clients
Clergy
Customers
Consultants
Educators
Employees
Government
Insurers
International customers
Management
Media
Social agencies
Stockholders

These very descriptions will help you know who your audiences are and what topics will interest them. Your lists will also help you determine when and how to reach them. To reach your business-to-business audience, trade newspapers and magazines will most likely be the most effective type of media. Topics will be business-related. Timing would be tied closely to the topic. For example, tax-related news should be timed before the end of the calendar year.

GET TO KNOW YOUR INTERNAL AUDIENCES

I worked for a local hospital for two years as a communications manager. One of the first projects I was given was to research the internal newsletter for improvements. It was time for an employee survey. I'll never forget the results of that survey.

To begin with, I was certain the format of the newsletter was a drawback. It was formatted in a nondescript way, using horizontal paragraphs on blue paper. I believed that changing the format would increase attention and readership. I truly expected that a better format would have been newspaper style on white or brighter paper. Being new to the company, I did not fully know the audience yet and made the mistake of assuming what the audience wanted.

The employees—per the returned surveys—liked the format of the newsletter and overwhelmingly voted to keep the layout as it was. The remainders of the answers were very scattered, and the only item of interest garnered from the survey was to keep the format.

Here's a face-it fact: Do NOT ever assume what your audience wants.

Your internal audience will always make the best marketers,

promoters, and supporters you can find. It is vital that you keep communications open, clear, and concise. To do that, you need the proper topics and the right timing, and you need to use the right type of media, formatted the way they want it.

DEFINING YOUR AUDIENCE—DEFINE YOUR TOPICS

For whatever reasons—financial, employment, consumer, or business-to-business—your audiences already have an interest in your company and its products or services. So your topic work can be almost complete by the time you have a good understanding of who your audiences are.

Your audience should be considered when applying all parts of the T-Connector Formula. In later chapters, you'll see how knowing your audience helps with timing and type of media.

For now, keep in mind that marketing, public relations, and advertising (or the T-Connector Formula) only work when directed toward the people who your company or organization services.

WHEN DEFINING YOUR AUDIENCES, REMEMBER TO…

The previous chapter listed the different types of audiences that will play an important role in your complete audience definitions. Chart 6.1 illustrates how all the dimensions of your target audience fit together.

Chart 6.1 Defining Target Audiences

<u>**Public Relations Plan's Definition of Target Audience**</u>

       Decision-maker   Persons using product or service

<u>**Characteristics of Audiences**</u>

       Demographics   Convinced or needs convinced

       Hostile or friendly   Preferred media

A FEW GOOD EXAMPLES

The New York Times online reported in January 2007 that 51 percent of women are living without a spouse in the United States. Does your audience fall in that group: living alone and liking it? If so, you have plenty of opportunities to address your audience about what your company can do for their current lifestyle choice.

Diets always seem to be in the big news of the day (everyday, actually). One of the latest diet craze is low carbohydrates, high protein. The American Egg Board runs ads in print and on television with a public relations-type message promoting eating eggs and adding protein to your diet.

The latest diet trend in 2008 is the lunchbox diet. It is based on a simple principle: Buy a large plastic lunchbox and fill it with a highly nutritious mix of 60 percent vegetables, 30 percent protein, and 10 percent fat. Throughout your day—possibly every hour—slowly graze on the lunchbox contents, and then you will be less likely to binge at mealtimes.

Why is this 'the' diet of 2008? Because the diet was featured in a super-stylish fashion magazine. Fast food restaurants jumped on the same healthier-eating bandwagon with new menus and new advertising, all aimed at healthy eating choices; imagine, you can now order fruit with your Big Mac. Food companies knew their audiences wanted healthy, lower-calorie foods, and they designed their communications to address that topic in the proper time frame.

It's all about emotion promotion…emotion commotions. What makes your audience think, act, feel, react, and believe? Find those answers and you'll find a wealth of topics that will create emotion, commotion, and effective promotion.

CHAPTER SEVEN

MEET THE SAMPLE COMPANIES

Ben Franklin was a printer by vocation and a scientist by avocation.

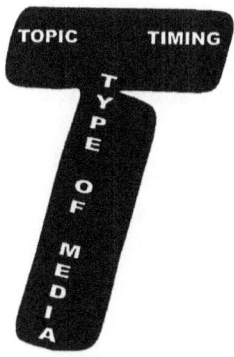

To better illustrate the way the T-Connector Formula works, this book will use two fictional companies. The first company, the Tree Top Company, is a retail landscape and gardening products and services company.

The second company is a not-for-profit organization called Community Educational Services. They provide adults with educational counseling services. The organization helps adults find a career path and then helps them apply to colleges, technical schools, or technical training. In addition to these services, they also help adults apply for educational funding in the form of grants, scholarships, or student loans.

HERE ARE THE FACTS

Each of the sample companies has many similarities and many

differences. Before we start applying the T-Connector Formula for the companies' promotional needs, we need to know a few facts about each company. We need to understand their history, their products and services, what their strengths are (unique positioning statements), and of course who their audiences are (both internal and external).

The following charts show you all the pertinent information about each company. Take a few minutes to look at them both.

TABLE 7.1

THE TREE TOP COMPANY

Years in Business	Starting twentieth year
Incorporated	Yes
Owned by	Two brothers
Number of employees	Thirty

Products offered

Trees	flowers
Gardening tools	
Fertilizers	pots
Ponds	indoor plants

Services offered

Retail sales
Landscape design
Gardening consulting
Mowing and trimming
Free lectures and seminars

Known for

Customer service
Unique plants
Research
Quality products and services
Community involvement

Audiences
Internal audience includes employees, suppliers, stockholders, and the owners. External audiences include homeowners between the ages of twenty-five and seventy with household incomes between $35,000 and $250,000 a year. Females are the main decision-makers.

TABLE 7.2

Community Educational Services

Years in business	Eight years
Grant funded	Community Grant
Board of directors	Eight from educational, business, and community
Number of employees	Fifteen

Services
Educational and career counseling for adults eighteen years and older
Help adults apply for grants and student loans

Known for
Customer service and a caring staff
Effective educational and career guidance
Research
A knowledge base
Partnerships with community and educational providers
Community involvement: hosts an education and job fair event twice a year

Audiences
Internal audiences include board members, employees, educational resources, and educational funding resources. External audiences include males and females between the ages of eighteen and forty, generally single. The organization does service a small percentage of nontraditional students who are married (males and females) with incomes below $35,000 a year that are looking to change careers. Over 80percent of the external audience is made up of persons who are trying to enter the job market for the first time or are trying to improve their skills for better job opportunities.

BOTH USE MARKETING AND PUBLIC RELATIONS PLANNING

Both of our sample companies use marketing and public relations to keep their internal and external audiences up-to-date with company news. Both companies have a combined department that works from one integrated marketing and public relations plan. Each company employs one marketing person and one public relations professional.

All avenues of marketing and public relations are considered and implemented as needed. As such, both companies use paid advertising, press releases, PSAs, local cable television, and print materials such as brochures, catalogs, posters, and flyers.

The Tree Top Company has an internal sales force of ten plant experts. The Community Educational Services uses eight consultants (who are called counselors) to do their sales. Both companies service a tri-county geographic area.

GOOD PRESS TOPICS FOR THE TREE TOP COMPANY

The next chapter will detail applying the topic part of the T-Connector Formula to the Tree Top Company; for now, let's take a quick look at some of the topic opportunities we can find based on the information we know about the company.

We can find that the Tree Top Company is ready to celebrate a twenty-year anniversary, a great opportunity for press releases and special advertising in print, radio, and television.

The free lectures are great topics for press releases, as are personnel changes or advancements. The company does research on new fertilizers, plants, landscape designs, and many other areas related to gardening. All of their research findings would make relevant press release topics. The company is involved in many community projects, such as donating trees for Arbor Day, hosting school tours in their facility, doing community talks, and giving holiday decorating seminars. Plus they support causes such as cancer, literacy, and nontraditional jobs for women.

Wow. This company is packed full of public relations opportunities as well as marketing and promotional topics.

Later chapters will look at timing and types of media that would work well for the Tree Top Company.

GOOD PRESS TOPICS FOR THE COMMUNITY EDUCATIONAL SERVICES ORGANIZATION

As a nonprofit organization, press releases, PSAs, and local cable talk shows are always appropriate. This company also has need for paid advertising, brochures, flyers, and other types of media that will be explored in a later chapter. As you'll soon learn, timing means a great deal to this company.

From a quick review of the company's facts, we can see immediate topics for feature articles, such as the partnerships with educational and funding resources, the updating of their knowledge base, personnel changes and advancements, new information about training and funding, and plenty of human interest stories.

A CLOSER LOOK

We will continue to learn more about both of the sample companies. As we do, we'll also learn ways to get each of the companies in the news so that they can promote, promote, promote.

Later chapters will follow the sample companies through timing and type of media. Topics for the sample company are detailed in the next chapter.

CHAPTER EIGHT

TOPIC AND THE SAMPLE COMPANIES

"Success is formula, not fantasy."
David Niven, Ph.D.

Time to see if the formula can be applied to our sample companies. This section will demonstrate how the topic part of the T-Connector Formula can be applied to the two sample companies, starting with the Tree Top Company.

THE TREE TOP COMPANY

Although this company is a for-profit organization, they have many areas that would fit a press release or a PSA. As stated earlier, this company really gets involved with the community. They donate trees to various community projects and company experts travel to different organizations in the community, including K-12 school districts, to give demonstrations and lectures on gardening, landscaping, and taking care of plants.

The company also keeps up on the latest gardening and planting trends through their research department. They also try to offer their customers the latest information about fertilizers and weed killers, all of which makes for good news to report to the audiences they serve.

It just so happens that the company is celebrating a twenty-year anniversary. They also offer year-round free lectures on gardening, seasonal planting and decorating, landscaping, and a variety of other topics. Of course there are plenty of personnel changes and advancements that they can report to the community at large.

Although there are many topics for press, this section will only look at two topics in particular. Let's look at the free lectures first, not because it is the most obvious but because the company offers one a month, which makes getting into press a monthly, year-round possibility. The lectures can also make good copy for the radio.

The seminars could also attract local or regional television because of the topics covered. They can also be adjusted to offer seasonal topics, which adds to the timing part of the T-Connector Formula. Here's an example:

"Twenty years in business is an accomplishment by any business standard and, as such, should be noted and celebrated. The Tree Top Company will be offering special purchases throughout the year along with several events. They will kick off the year with a special free-to-the-public open house." Lots of press opportunities here.

COMMUNITY EDUCATIONAL SERVICES

For local news, this organization can do a regular feature, once or twice a year, on educational trends, both locally and nationally. They can report on new funding and on new educational courses and resources they are working with. Twice yearly, they host an educational and job fair.

The educational and job fair creates news for press releases, PSAs, talk show topics, not to mention the flyers, posters, and information sheets that can be distributed throughout the community. The organization also schedules both print and broadcast media buys for the event.

Staff promotions and additions are all reportable. New and retiring board members, special donations, and all associations with community events are considered newsworthy and reportable. They are also launching a Web site, which is always newsworthy (for now anyway).

SAMPLE PRESS RELEASE FOR THE TREE TOP COMPANY

Let's try a sample press release for the Tree Top Company. We'll use their regularly scheduled holiday seminar as the topic.

**** NEWS RELEASE****
IMMEDIATE RELEASE

DATE: _____
CONTACT: Joe Smith, Public Relations, 555-555-5555

ANYTOWN, USA: The Tree Top Company will be hosting a free seminar on December 3 at 1 p.m. in the Big Fir lecture room. The free talk will discuss selecting, caring for, and growing holiday evergreens. Free information and fact sheets will be given to all in attendance and time for questions will be available at the end of the lecture. The Tree Top Company is a full-service landscaping firm offering design, layout, planting, and retail sales. Tree Top's lecture hall is located at 5555 Tree Top Lane.

For more information or to register, call 555-555-5555.
###

Press releases should always be printed on company letterhead. Now that we have one press release with a selected topic, we'll look at the timing and type of media in later chapters. For now, using the free lecture as the topic, let's write out a PSA for radio broadcast.

PSA FOR THE TREE TOP COMPANY
**** NEWS RELEASE****
      IMMEDIATE RELEASE

DATE: _____
CONTACT: Joe Smith, Public Relations, 555-555-5555

Are you getting ready to buy your holiday evergreens? Would you like to learn how to select the proper evergreen for your needs? Would you also like to know how to properly care for them after you've made the commitment and the purchase?

Tis the season not to panic. The Tree Top Company is hosting a free seminar on December 3rd at 1 p.m. in the Big Fir lecture room. The free talk will discuss selecting, caring for, and growing holiday evergreens.

Information and fact sheets will be given to all in attendance and time for questions will be available at the end of the lecture. The Tree Top Company is located at 5555 Tree Top Lane. For more information or to register, call 555-555-55-55.

PSAs, remember, are written in the first person. All the Ws and the Ps are in each of the releases. Let's look at a press release announcing the twentieth-year celebration. The company will be hosting an open house on February 14. This event will be the kick-off event for the yearlong celebration. Following is the press release and the PSA.

DATE: _____
CONTACT: Joe Smith, Public Relations, 555-555-5555

ANYTOWN, USA: It is only December and you already have a date for Valentine's Day, February 14. The Tree Top Company will be hosting an open house to kick off their yearlong celebration of twenty years in business.

There will be free chocolates, free roses, and surprise guest speakers throughout the day. If you have gardening questions or would like to learn what you should be doing for spring planting season, join us at this customer appreciation open house on February 14 from 10 a.m. to 4 p.m.

The Tree Top Company is a full-service landscaping firm offering design, layout, planting, and retail sales. They are located at 5555 Tree Top Lane. For more information about the upcoming open house, call 555-555-5555.

###

Here is the PSA:
**** NEWS RELEASE****
            IMMEDIATE RELEASE

DATE: _____
CONTACT: Joe Smith, Public Relations, 555-555-5555

ANYTOWN, USA: Valentine's Day is a good day to celebrate being together. Come to the Tree Top Company on February 14 to help us celebrate serving the community for twenty years. The Tree Top Company will be hosting an open house to kick off their yearlong twentieth anniversary.

And, since it is Valentine's Day, there will be free chocolates, free roses, and surprise guest speakers throughout the day. If you have gardening questions or would like to learn what you should be doing for spring planting season, join us at this customer appreciation open house on February 14 from 10 a.m. to 4 p.m.

The Tree Top Company is located at 5555 Tree Top Lane. For more information about the upcoming open house, call 555-555-5555.
                              ###

SAMPLE PRESS RELEASE FOR COMMUNITY EDUCATIONAL SERVICES

For today, the organization's new Web site is newsworthy.
**** NEWS RELEASE****
IMMEDIATE RELEASE

DATE: _____
CONTACT: Janet Smith, Public Relations, 555-555-5554

ANYTOWN, USA: Community Educational Services announced that they will officially launch www.commedservices.org on June 15, 2002.

The new Web site is the official online site for the educational counseling service. Adults wishing to return or enter college, adult education, or technical schools can log onto the site 24/7 to view class listings, educational sites, and providers. Online users can also print a student loan application and set up an appointment to speak with an educational counselor.

Jan Miller, director of Community Educational Services, said, "The site will help serve the adults in northeast Ohio more effectively and much more quickly than calling in or stopping in the office. Persons viewing the site can take their time and view the available information before coming in to speak to a counselor."

For more information, call Community Educational Services at 555-555-5555 or log onto www.commedservices.org.

###

PSA FOR THE COMMUNITY EDUCATIONAL SERVICES
**** NEWS RELEASE****
IMMEDIATE RELEASE

DATE: _____
CONTACT: Janet Smith, Public Relations, 555-555-5554

It is never too late to educate! If you have been thinking about returning to school for a college degree or technical certification, we have a Web site just for you.

Log onto to www.commedservices.org for the latest information on class listings, educational sites, and providers. Online users can also print a student loan application and set up an appointment to speak with an educational counselor.

For more information, call Community Educational Services at 555-555-5555 or start surfing at www.commedservices.org.

###

Again, all the Ws and Ps and the mechanics are in place. The only thing missing is the date on each release. We have not determined timing as yet so we will look at setting dates in a later chapter.

Now we have topics for each of the sample companies that are versatile enough to adapt to both print and broadcast. In later chapters, we will look at when each of the releases and PSAs should be sent and to whom.

CHAPTER NINE

TIMING

"I have sometimes almost wished it had been
my destiny to be born two or three centuries hence."
Benjamin Franklin

Timing is everything. Timing can make or break a joke. Timing can make or break a great room entrance. Watch any of the film and television award shows and it's easy to see how important big entrances are to Hollywood stars. Part of a publicists job is to time a star's entrance perfectly so that the room is full of people or photographers and journalists waiting to witness the entrance. Timing.

Buying shares of Enron stock was a good investment in September of 2001, but not so good in September 2002. Timing.

To get a clear photograph of a rainbow curved across an ocean-lined horizon depends on timing. One has to be at the ocean during a sun-streaked rainy afternoon. The camera has to be loaded with film and focused, and the shutter has to be timed correctly to capture the rainbow. All a matter of timing.

The 2008 Summer Olympic gold medal winner, Michael Phelps won his 100-meter butterfly gold by one one-hundreth of a second. Talk about good timing.

Good timing produces good results. Getting the company's news to the media before their deadline, at a relevant time of the year, and related to the big news of the day can produce consistently publicized news.

David Yale wrote in *The Publicity Handbook*, "The right timing for your product publicity is critical. In addition to conforming to media lead times, you have to determine if the marketplace needs to be "conditioned" ahead of time to accept publicity for a product that people may not even have thought of."

DEADLINES—DEADLINES—DEADLINES

Remember, reporters from all types of media live and die by deadlines. What are their deadlines? Call them and ask.

Adhere to their deadlines. When a reporter calls your company with a question for an article or interview, always ask, "What is your deadline?"

Make sure you call the reporter back before their deadline with some sort of response, even if it is just to say that you are still working on it.

TIMING IS MORE THAN MEETING DEADLINES

Although meeting the media's deadline is the most important aspect of the timing part of the T-Connector Formula, timing does hold other meanings as well.

Timing can refer to:

1. The proper day of the week and the right time of the day to send releases and PSAs. Friday at 4:45 p.m. is not a good time to send information to the press. More than likely it will not receive a lot of attention until the following Monday, and who knows what can happen to the information between Friday night and Monday morning? Wednesday mornings are reportedly slower news days than the rest of the week.

2. Fitting the topic to the seasonal time of the year or any local community events. Back to school, any of the holidays, participation in outdoor community events, bicycle safety awareness month, literacy month, stroke awareness month, fall, summer, beat the winter blahs; these are just a few examples that can help you fit your message to the time of the year.

3. Make it relevant to the reader. On every release ask yourself why the information needs to get to the audience or the reader. And, why does the reader need to know at this particular time? Bad, or good, economic times are part of the big news every day. Training companies can publicize new training classes, report trends in

training, or show a relationship between a lower unemployment rate and higher educated employees.

4. Getting the information to the media in plenty of time (call and ask the media source to define their version of "plenty of time" for you) to be included in any special reporting sections such as the food section, the living section, or any other relevant sections that may be reported on a weekly, monthly, or semi-annual basis.

KNOW THE MEDIA AND WHAT THEY WANT TO KNOW

Many organizations complain that they just can't get good media coverage no matter what they do. The media doesn't understand their type of industry or business, or the media just doesn't "get" the company's mission. If that is true, it becomes the responsibility of the company to help the media understand what it is trying to accomplish and why the company's news is important to the community.

Company representatives should call and set up a meeting, confirm the dates and times, and bring a media or press kit to the meeting. The media really does have limited space and time, and the entire community is competing for it. You get a sense of how big a community is when competing with other organizations for media coverage.

Of course, you have a relevant topic, but timing is also critical. Spring 2002 brought a level 2 tornado through parts of northeast Ohio.

Luckily there were no deaths and only minor injuries but property damage was extensive. For the next week to ten days, the papers, the radio, and regional television mainly covered the property damage and rightly so.

Property damage is what interested the community during that time, and that is exactly what the media delivered. There were press releases on other topics and there were even a few features covering topics other than the tornado. More or less, the papers were filled front to back, top to bottom with news about the tragic Sunday afternoon filled with unexpected stormy weather.

Timing was bad that week to try to contact a reporter to do any secondary coverage. The big news took control.

WHAT TAKES UP ALL THE TIME AND SPACE

It is vital to get to know the sections of all of your local newspapers, trade magazines, local and regional magazines, and local radio and television shows.

For example, most local or regional newspapers include the following sections:

- Breaking and hard news (usually front page and first section)
- Sports
- Business news
- Community or local news

- Arts and living

- Food news

- Travel

- Human interest

- Special features

- Classified

- Real estate

- Home and garden

Food may only be reported once a week (maybe on Wednesdays). Arts and living may only appear in Friday's issue. With the baby-boomers becoming the new senior crowd, many newspapers or regional magazines do in-depth coverage two or three times a year on what is important to senior citizens. Can you fit a feature or press releases in with that topic at that time of the year? If so, know when to get the information to the media in time for their features.

A FEW GOOD EXAMPLES ARE IN ORDER

In 2001–2002 the economy took a downturn and many layoffs occurred. In northeast Ohio, one of the industries hit the worst was the steel industry. That was the big news of the time. For an organization promoting adult education, GED, or adult technical training, this was a good time to send press releases to inform the laid-off workers in the area that education can and does make a difference.

A good lead might go like this:

In today's job market, education is more important than ever.

There are adult education classes available nationwide to teach non-English-speaking adults how to read, write, and speak English. Organizations promoting such classes can watch for new businesses in their areas that are newly hiring non-English-speaking employees and do a direct mail campaign to them, promoting their classes. Press releases could also be geared toward employers that have a large number of non-English-speaking employees. Diversity training could also be promoted to the same people in the same manner.

Every area in the country has a back-to-school season. This is perfect timing to run press releases on safety tips, health tips, or any special after-school services. In the fall of 2001, kids carrying backpacks became a hot topic. Backpack manufacturers, schools, healthcare facilities, and orthopedic-related service companies all ran public service announcements and press releases regarding the best way to wear a backpack, what to carry in a backpack, the weight ratio between the child and the backpack, and ways to mend health problems created from carrying backpacks.

Another annual event is New Year's. Editors will be seeking features on looking back at the previous year and looking forward to the next year. If your company can pitch a feature timed for the new year, you should do so in November for dailies, weeklies, and August or

September for monthlies and trade and consumer magazines.

TIMING YOUR INFORMATION TO THE READER'S BEST INTEREST

Timing is everything. Reward is just. Timing your organization's news to the big news of the day allows you to put your reader's interest first. Your number one priority in business is to provide products and services to benefit your customer. By timing your news to the reader's best interest, the reader will immediately see the benefit in reading your news and ultimately acting upon it.

In September 2002, Jerry Brown's *Monday Morning Minute* newsletter reported the following about timing your story to one of the major story themes of the day: "With corporate and church scandals, the war on terrorism and a busy wildfire season in the western United States, we don't seem to have those [slow news days] anymore. Does that mean you have to put your feature stories on the shelf for now? Not if you can find a way to tie your story to one of the major story themes playing out in the media these days."

WORKING WITH A MEDIA CALENDAR

Setting the timing can be planned and plugged into a calendar— a media calendar, that is. If you have services or products that can take on a seasonal theme, you can calendar those topics into your media calendar, often a year in advance. If your company or organization holds annual events that are free and open to the general public, put them on the media calendar as soon as you know the exact dates of the events. Although the event(s) may be scheduled for a particular date, your media calendar should show press releases, advertising, and radio PSAs at least four to six weeks in advance of the event. Again, all part of the timing.

The media calendar is an important part of your marketing and public relations plan. You can use an electronic or software-based calendar, a year-long planner (one of the hundreds of free calendars you receive as a promotional gift from the myriad of vendors you do business with), or any type of month-to-month list. No matter the format, a media calendar will help you plan the messages you'll send throughout the year. One management tip for maintaining an effective media calendar: Always keep room on the media calendar for unexpected events and news releases.

NO TIME LIKE THE PRESENT

Both sample companies keep and follow a yearlong media calendar to help manage and implement timing. Both companies plan ahead for seasonally themed releases and advertising. After looking at how the sample companies use timing, types of media will be explained.

CHAPTER TEN

AUDIENCE AND TIMING

"His first effort was to maximize his horse's exposure…"
Laura Hillenbrand
Seabiscuit: An American Legend

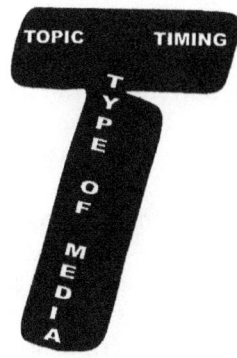

Timing, as discussed earlier, refers to timing the topic to the big news of the day, giving your message a seasonal theme, or meeting the media's deadlines. The same can be said when timing your news to your audiences' schedules.

KNOW WHEN THY AUDIENCE IS LISTENING OR READING

Chapter Six detailed how to learn about your audience, how to determine what is relevant to your audience, and how to develop topics for your audience. Timing and your audience relates to knowing when your audiences are available to hear, read, or see the news from your company.

Are you trying to reach teachers? If so, is the best time to reach them during the school year or during their time off? Better find out before you send your news.

Does your news relate to afternoon shift manufacturing employees? If so, don't put your news on during the morning drive time or the 6:00 p.m. news.

Do you know why daytime dramas have been tagged "soap operas"? Because detergent makers used to sponsor most of the shows and the detergent companies wanted to reach homemakers and stay-at-home moms. Their research showed that the afternoon was the best time to do this so they have been longtime sponsors of daytime dramas.

TIMING YOUR TOPIC TO YOUR AUDIENCE

Public relations, promotion, and marketing are used in some form in every type of business. Whether people admit it or not, they are drawn to any news that relates to the big news of the day. Your audiences will more than likely have an active stake in what is happening around them.

A good example of relating your company's news to the big news of the day—specifically for your audiences—is Charles Howard, the owner of Seabiscuit. In researching the life of the famous racehorse for her book, Laura Hillenbrand's found that as Seabiscuit started beating the odds and winning races, Howard needed to maximize the horse's exposure.

Howard practically lived with reporters during the times that Seabiscuit was racing. According to Hillenbrand's research, Howard made himself available before and after races to the press for questions. Howard knew the country wanted to hear and read about how an underdog ("underhorse") came through to be a winner.

The country had just come through the worst ten years of its history, the Depression. Horse racing started to emerge as a favorite pastime, and people across the country were reading and listening to radio broadcasts about horse races.

The country needed a little guy to make it big, and they found that in Seabiscuit. Because of Howard and his press-related efforts, his undersized, crooked-legged, underdog racehorse got more newspaper column inches in 1938 than Hitler, Howard Hughes, Clark Gable, or the pope, according to Hillenbrand's book, *Seabiscuit: An American Legend*.

Charles Howard knew his audience, knew what they wanted to hear, knew where they wanted to hear it or read it, and used all those factors to present his horse's story to the country. As such, Seabiscuit was one of the most well-known horses, and Seabiscuit's story is the most well told and most often told horse story in history.

THEME YOUR NEWS RELEASES TO YOUR AUDIENCE

Are your audiences most reachable during the holidays? Maybe your audiences are most accessible during elections or during the summer.

In adult education, adult students are conditioned to think about registration during specific times of the year, such as during August and September. It is most effective to reach them during this time to encourage those considering registering to register. Or, it is a great time to publish information critical to registration, such as tuition hikes.

Does your company participate or market to deer hunters (fall theme), engaged couples (spring theme for spring weddings), or family vacationers (summer theme)? There are all kinds of themes attached to all of these events.

MEET MEDIA DEADLINES...MEET YOUR AUDIENCES' DEADLINES

To make the topics fit, you have to get your information to the desired media according to their deadlines and your audiences' deadlines.

If you want to reach adults before they register for fall classes, you need to get your news releases, PSAs, Web site information, ezine news, or television appearances scheduled and completed in plenty of time to reach the students.

CHAPTER ELEVEN

TIMING AND THE SAMPLE COMPANIES

*"Failure is not trying. The fear of failure is powerful.
...Not trying is, of course, the ultimate failure..."*
#63 of The 100 Simple Secrets
of Successful People

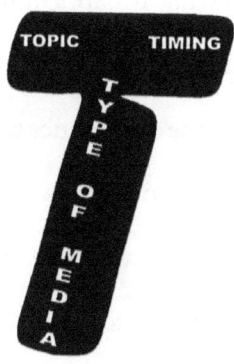

The Tree Top Company would, of course, have the proper setting to plan and calendar its free seminars six to twelve months in advance. Seminars are built on topics such as growing seasons or plants related to the time of the year. For example, seminars may have titles such as "How to select, plant, and care for that special evergreen during the holiday season" or "Tips on planting a springtime garden."

The company has topics list and seasonal relationships. The other timing consideration is that the releases need to be to the media two to six weeks before each event.

Community Educational Services also has seasonal events that can be calendared six to twelve months in advance. Educational and job fairs, return to school in the fall reminders, or summertime preparation for fall information can be used in press releases.

MONITORING THE ENVIRONMENT

The public relations and marketing professionals at both companies read the local, regional, and national newspapers and trade papers to keep current with what is happening, both in their own fields and in general throughout the community.

Local layoffs would make a difference to Community Educational Services. Tuition increases, announcements made from area colleges, new careers, and new industries in the area are topics from the community that would interest Community Educational Services.

New or slow construction in the area would interest the Tree Top Company, as would forest fires, new parks or school programs, employment predictions for horticulture or colleges, and technical school news regarding horticulture.

Timing press releases to address the same issues and needs expressed by others in the community would help increase the likelihood of press releases and PSAs published from our two sample companies.

TIMING FOR THE SAMPLES

Back in Chapter Seven, we developed press releases for the Tree Top Company announcing a free lecture on holiday evergreens and promoting their twenty-year anniversary event. Let's start with the lecture date. If the lecture is scheduled for December 3, to ensure proper press coverage and publication of the press release, the company should start sending the release at least four to eight weeks in advance: late October. If they are sending to local monthly publications, four to five weeks is sufficient time to get to the media before the deadline.

Trade publications should receive the release as much as two months in advance. Again, it is best to contact each publication for specific deadlines.

The release should be sent to weekly and daily publications at least two to three weeks in advance of each of those publication deadlines. The PSA we developed can be sent several days to a week in advance of the event.

Timing for the twenty-year open house should also be sent to the monthly publications four to eight weeks in advance of the event date. It should be sent two to three weeks in advance for weeklies and dailies. Radio commercial buys should happen at least a month in advance and carry through up to the day before the event.

Community Educational Services' event was scheduled for June 15. Same scheduling applies for this release, starting in early May (monthly publications) and continuing through early June (for weekly and daily publications). The new Web site would be of interest to those reading the trade magazines, so the organization needs to send the release to trade publications up to two months prior to the launch of the

Web site.

TYPE OF MEDIA AND WE ARE SET TO GO

We have the topics, we have the timing, now we need a list of media to send to. We have alluded to several already, but we will define specifics in a later chapter.

CHAPTER TWELVE

TYPE OF MEDIA

"All the news that's fit to print."
The New York Times

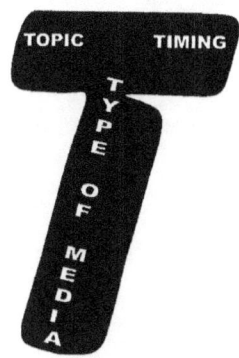

The tower of the T-Connector, type of media, contributes the final factor to the media connection equation. This chapter introduces the various types of media; all of the standards are listed, as well as a few overlooked outlets that are just as effective as the standards.

TIME TO THINK ABOUT SELECTING THE TYPE OF MEDIA

You will soon notice that this section supplies more questions than answers. An effective way to determine the kind of media to use for your topic or message is to answer all of the questions below:

1. What audience are you trying to reach and which media will best reach that audience? For example, perhaps this audience listens to rock radio stations, or maybe they watch the local television

news more often than they listen to a radio.

2. When is the audience most accessible: in the morning, in the evening, after school?

3. How much can you spend to reach the audience?

4. Which type of media has the highest credibility with your audience?

5. Which type of media can deliver the topic or message in the time frame your audience needs to hear it?

6. Do you need to use more than one type of media to reach the audience?

Now that you started thinking about those answers, let's get some help by exploring the four media Ps of promotion; then we list the different categories of media. Tips on how to find the media in a particular area, and developing, using, and maintaining a media list, will also be detailed in this section.

FOUR Ps OF MEDIA PROMOTION

Before looking at the different types of media, a brief description of the different media promotion types are in order, or the 4Ps of media promotion:

Press Releases: Sent to newspapers, magazines, newsletters, trade publications, Web site publications, or any type of print media.

PSAs: Sent to radio and television stations or any type of broadcast media.

Promotional Print Advertising: Ads, brochures, flyers, fact sheets, press kits, promotional giveaways such as pens and pencils, mailers, and other types of printed material used for promotion.

Posters/Bulletin Boards/Interactive Media: Posters, Web site banners, Web sites, CD-ROM promotion.

Each of these media Ps of promotion fit a different type of media outlet, which is the first step in determining the type of media that fits the topic and the timing.

LIST OF MEDIA TYPES

An average person going through everyday life is exposed to hundreds of promotional messages each and every day. Television and radio commercials, print ads, outdoor billboards, point-of-purchase displays, store windows, supermarket shopping carts, on-hold messages, posters on trains and buses, place cards on taxis, you can even find advertising on the coffee cup you use every morning in your local diner. Have you noticed how much advertising you are exposed to when pumping gas for your car these days?

Media types, forms, outlets—whatever name you give it—would fill a dictionary-size book if they were all listed. This section attempts to provide a list of the basic structures or categories of media. Without further ado, here are the types of media and a few high points of each.

TELEVISION

Send public service announcements, video news releases, satellite media tours.

Opportunities include news programs, public affairs programs, talk shows, feature segments, and scrolling community calendars on local cable or public access channels.

Network television (ABC, NBC, FOX, CBS)
Regional network television (major stations in major cities such as Cleveland or Columbus)
Syndication television
Spot or local cable television (market-by-market, non-network and non-syndication)
Network cable television (pay channels, pay-per-view, basic cable)
Regional cable television

RADIO

Send public service announcements, audio news releases, and offer radio media tours.

There are over 9,000 commercial radio stations. Radio's reach is broader than newspapers or magazines. People have radios on at work, at home, and in their car. Radio can be heard on public transportation systems and in waiting rooms or lobbies.

Network radio and syndication radio
Spot or local radio

MAGAZINES

Send press releases via fax, mail, email.

There are over 2,000 consumer magazines available today. Categories include:

National
Consumer
Trade
Regional
Local
Entertainment

NEWSPAPERS

Send press releases via fax, mail, email.

Most newspapers are available in print and online. The over-fifty crowd tends to read the print version, whereas the under-thirty crowd is turning to online news.

National (*USA Today, Wall Street Journal,* and *Christian Science Monitor*)
Regional (major newspapers in the major cities)
Local: Daily, weekly, monthly publications
Specialized

OUT-OF-HOME MEDIA

This list is so vast that it is impossible to provide in a complete form. A few items listed below may not come to mind as quickly as other types of media.

Video, corporate, presentational, video conferencing
Film
Slide presentations
Displays and exhibits
Posters
Billboards
Bulletin boards
Movie theater preview
Bus signs
Shopping carts

Bike racks
Sports programming advertising
Coffee cups
Napkins
Menus

INTERACTIVE MEDIA

Includes Webcasting, online news distribution, online monitoring.

The Web
Email
U.S. mail
CD-ROM/DVD
Fax machine
Home shopping television and Internet
Telephone marketing
Speaker's bureaus
Presentations

MISCELLANEOUS

Again this list is endless, but here are a few samples to get you thinking.

T-shirts, pens, pencils, and other types of custom-printed giveaways
Direct mail campaigns
Newsletters
Catalogs
Remote radio broadcasts
Tickets to sporting events
Cars, trucks, buses

There's the sampling list. Remember, it is only the tip of the iceberg but it is a great start for someone new to public relations and marketing. Finding new media outlets in your company's demographics remains a constant task that requires keeping your eyes and ears open to new types of media.

WHERE ARE THE MEDIA?

The media seem to be everywhere these days, except where we want them to be. How do you find the hundreds of local newspapers, magazines, and cable shows in the area? Start with the local bookstores, libraries, newsstands, lobbies, waiting areas, stores, and of course the Internet.

As always, a wealth of information is available on the Internet. Start by visiting the sites listed below. Each of these sites is a search engine that is used to find other Web sites.

- google.com
- yahoo.com
- lycos.com
- hotbot.com
- radiolocator.com
- sendlistinfo@netscape.net (this is an email address where you can request a list of specialized media to buy, such as sports media, top 100 newspapers, local TV news, etc.)

After entering "newspapers" in the search criteria, narrow the search by following the screen prompts to enter a geographic location. For example, to find newspapers in the Columbus, Ohio area, go to yahoo. com. Enter the words "newspapers in Columbus, Ohio" in the search box, click on the Search button. If you replace "Columbus, Ohio" with your geographic area, within seconds you should see a list of newspapers in the area.

MEDIA LISTS

Media lists are just that, lists of media. Media lists can be kept as a printed catalog, or maintained in database software, saved in a word processor file, managed with contact management software, or saved in your email program. The purpose of a media list is to organize the media resources your company uses on a regular basis. The list or lists should be easily accessible for daily use.

A media list can be broken down into categories such as type (print, broadcast, webcast, etc.), publication cycle (weeklies, monthlies, dailies), or whatever manner that will provide the quickest and easiest access when sending press releases or PSAs or when calling to pitch a story for a feature.

However you keep the media list, or however it is broken down and organized, the list should always contain the following:

+ Publication name
+ Contact name (editor's names)
+ Contact names (reporters and topics they cover)
+ Address
+ Phone
+ Fax
+ Email addresses
+ Whether the editors like press releases faxed, mailed, or emailed
+ Deadlines
+ Call letters
+ Formats or specialties such as country western or classical music for radio stations or readers over fifty-five for publications, etc.

BUILDING AND MAINTAINING MEDIA LISTS

Continually scan the environment for new media starting up in the area or for those that you yourself may not read or listen to but your target audiences may frequent. Talk to your audience and ask what they are reading and listening to. Immediately add the answers to your media list.

Read regional and national newspapers at least two times a week. Peruse all types of magazines. By way of example, bird watching may or may not be your hobby, but it may pay off to look at a bird watching magazine every now and then to see if your company's information fits the media or you can pick up ideas for news releases.

TIPS ON GETTING TO KNOW THE MEDIA

There is only one way to get to know the media you will be using regularly, and that is to read, listen, or watch on a regular basis. Don't expect the media to want to get to know your organization when you don't know the media.

Keep in mind that media people don't automatically know everything just because they are in the media business. You may think they are watching your every move, but in reality they are hoping that you call and inform them.

The media do NOT have magic antennas that pick up news and information from behind closed corporate doors. There are laws against such actions. You tell and inform the media about your company through press releases and good media relations.

The tips listed below will help you.

1. Call the local media. Call the editors. Explain who you are, explain who your company is, and explain the organization's mission. Ask for their suggestions on what type of information their readers would like to know about. Get to know the editors and let the editors know you.

2. Get to know the local columnists and what they write about (and when).

3. Get to know the different sections of the publications and know who writes for each. A local daily newspaper has a living section, a local news section, an education reporter, a medical news reporter, an entertainment section, and sports and business sections. The newspaper also has a number of regular weekly columnists, each column covering a different topic such as volunteers, about town, general thoughts and opinions, and a humorist.

4. Scan the local cable channels for talk shows that highlight the geographic area of your audience. Call the talk show producers and ask how to get on their shows.

5. Look at, read, listen to, and peruse all ads, brochures, radio news spots, and community calendars. Learn from them. Copy them in terms of length, attitude, format, etc.

Everyone complains about the media and the intrusive manner in which they seem to operate. Nonetheless, everyone turns to the media to relay the "good news." To establish a good mutual trusting relationship with any media type, the media has to be respected for both sides of their persona.

Michael Levine offers the "Ten Commandments for Dealing with Media" in the *Guerrilla P.R. 2.0* which includes never being boring, knowing your subject, knowing the media contacts, reading the papers or watching the television shows, following up and following through, being persistent, covering your bases, thinking a few steps ahead and not taking it all so seriously.

SELECTING THE RIGHT MEDIA TYPES

The topic is selected, the timing is good, you know your media options; how do you know the best type of media to select? Following are a few more questions you'll want to answer before selecting the "who" and "what" media types:

1. Start with details about the audience: Is the audience general or specific?

2. If specific, can you reach them through local media only, regional, national, or Internet-based media?

3. Can the audience be reached through mass media such as television, radio, magazines, newspapers, wire services,

syndication, or columnists?

4. If you are trying to reach a specialized consumer market, can they be reached better by using special interest television, radio, magazines, or newspapers? You might want to consider direct mail.

5. For specialized audiences like business, educational, medical, or government, would it be beneficial to use business-, educational-, medical-, or government-related television (national or local), radio (national or local), newspapers, magazines, trade publications, columnists, or newsletters?

6. Is the audience made up of Internet-based readers and users?

ALL PARTS ARE IN LINE

The equation is complete: topic, timing, and type of media. The next chapter shows how the sample companies select their type of media for maximum effectiveness.

CHAPTER THIRTEEN

MORE ABOUT THE INTERNET MEDIA

"Cyberspace could become the carrier common to all, competing in all arenas—format, content, and distribution."
Rocking the Ages
J. Walker Smith and Ann Clurman

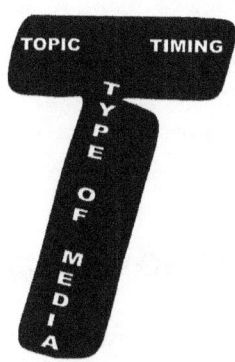

When people first started surfing the net, nobody was certain how big the waves would get. The heaviest users were the universities and the techies. Usage rapidly expanded to general consumers, students, hobbyists, and twenty-, thirty-, forty-, and eighty-something's.

You can now get Internet access almost everywhere these days. You can hookup (to the net) in restaurants, hotels, coffee shops, bookstores, and your local libraries. We spent a warm and sunny vacation in Cancun, Mexico, last year and the hotel had two computers in the lobby for the guests to check their email or stock prices. A coworker checked her office email while vacationing in Spain and Hawaii. Wow!

Face it. The Internet is an accepted medium for news, shopping, research, public relations, marketing, staying connected, and instant access to the world. Using the Internet for public relations, marketing, and communications requires research, planning, and constant updating.

Will the Internet work for your company or organization? Turn to your demographics to answer that question. Are your audiences using the net today? Will they be using it tomorrow or five years from now? A good resource for U.S. Web site usage and traffic statistics is online at cyberatlas.internet.com. Let's look at some general cyberspace demographics.

THIRTY-, FORTY-, FIFTY-SOMETHINGS

These age groups are most assuredly using the net, especially the thirty- and forty-something's. What are they using the net for? More importantly, if your company has thirty- and forty-something's in your target audiences, what are they using the net for?

TEENS AND TWENTY-SOMETHINGS

Both of these groups use the net extensively. Again, seriously, what do they use the net for? My twenty-something son and the majority of his friends never read the actual newspaper. They always get their news online. They search classified ads, job boards, business news, and sports all online. He and his friends can't even tell me the cost of a daily newspaper.

If these age groups are part of your audience, your news better fit this type of media.

GETTING THE NEWS 24/7

Just one of the reasons so many people use the Internet is that you can get news 24/7. All of my computers have the homepage set at www.newyorktimes.com. You'll learn how much I love this news source in a later chapter. For now, I bring it up because the *New York Times* Web site updates its online front page several times throughout the day. When something major happens somewhere in the world, I can get a quick update from www.newyorktimes.com.

That is the beauty of the net. The news is now available 24/7 from anywhere, about anything. Also, news and other Internet action are available via cell phones. News is becoming more instant and more attainable than ever before.

What does all this mean to your company and getting your company's news to your audiences? How do you apply the T-Connector Formula to this type of media?

ADVERTISING, PROMOTING, MARKETING, AND PUBLIC RELATIONS ON THE NET

The opportunities of using the Internet for advertising, promotion, marketing, and public relations are overwhelming. You can use ezines, Web sites, message boards, newsgroups, and list servers.

A slew of news is available on the thousands of blogs that have proliferated the net. News bloggers are writing all kinds of news on all kinds of topics at all kinds of news blogs.

Visit news.cnet.com or topbloglists.com for a sampling of the news blog sites live on the net today.

EZINES OR ENEWSLETTERS

Ezines and enewsletters are newsletters and magazines that are online at Web sites or emailed by request to readers. You can find hundreds of ezines on the net by using one of the search engines listed earlier; just search for "ezines." It is a good idea to review this type of media pretty thoroughly before using it.

USING YOUR WEB SITE TO GET YOUR NEWS OUT

Using your Web site as an interactive, informative type of media can be beneficial and help you justify the cost of the site. You can create topics in a timely manner and use the site as a type of media.

It is important to change your Web site regularly; you can use it to report all the news from your company. Use photos but keep the news section or press release section to the point and free of fluffed-up photos or graphics.

MESSAGE BOARDS

Message boards can be used to show off your expertise and to post expert help and advice on a specific topic. Reporters have been known to peruse messages boards for expert interviews.

NEWSGROUPS

Newsgroups generally are created to center on one basic subject.

Those interested in that subject may exchange messages and ideas. The messages are similar to email but are arranged or divided by topics.

LIST SERVERS

List servers work best for organizations advocating a cause; they can be used to promote your participation and support of said cause. List servers, much like message boards and newsgroups, are best used to discuss specific topics and problems. You can use all of these resources to network with others, solve problems, and show how your company is willing and able to be involved.

WHAT THE INTERNET MEANS TO THE T-CONNECTOR FORMULA

The T-Connector Formula can effectively be applied when determining the topic, the timing, and the type of Internet resource to use. Again, know your audience and how and when they use the net. Are your eighty-something's online to get the latest medical news or information? Is your target audience using list servers to get that information, or do they use the search engines? Are they surfing on Saturdays only?

These are all details you need to know to effectively place your news on the Internet. These same details fit the formula to a T.

CHAPTER FOURTEEN

MORE ABOUT BROADCAST MEDIA

*"Everything used to be so simple. There was television and there was radio.
One had pictures and one didn't. One had a few newscasts a day;
the other had a newscast at the top of every hour."*
Brad Kalbfeld

Associated Press
Broadcast News Handbook

The most alluring media type is broadcast media, especially television. Everyone wants television coverage. But, does every company belong on television?

You'll want to make sure your company can handle the traffic generated by television or radio. Does your company have a well-planned presentation with an effective spokesperson who is comfortable with speaking on radio or appearing on television? If not, you might want to research broadcast media presentations and get prepared before you get aired.

A STAR (OR TWO) IS BORN

All right, so you are certain that your company is ready for television; how do you get there, and can the T-Connector Formula help?

To catch the attention of television, you need a good, solid, relevant topic, and it needs to be timely. News becomes old faster on television than just about any other medium, including the Internet.

The best way to present to television is by using a pitch letter versus using a press release or PSA. Pitch letters are used to sell the idea. Press releases are used mainly to convey information. When using pitch letters, you need to have an attention-getting lead.

The letters are generally written in clear, straightforward language and should also include supporting data.

FINDING THE TOPICS OF INTEREST

Broadcast media, more than other type, needs to be studied closely for content and programming. Do you want to pitch to *Good Morning America*? Watch the show for several weeks and write down all the topics they present.

Your topic for the show must interest the producers, but don't forget to keep your target audience's interest in mind too. If you present a topic that is interesting to *Good Morning America* but offends your key groups, then you have misused broadcast media.

TIMING IS CRITICAL TO BROADCAST MEDIA

This type of news has to be on target to what is relevant to the rest of the world. Viewers expect instant gratification for giving their time to your presentation. If the audience has been hearing about cold and flu topics for the past four months and spring is fast approaching, they do not want you to continue to talk about cold and flu. They want sun and fun topics.

GENERAL BROADCAST MEDIA STATS TO THINK ABOUT

Who is watching and who is listening? In his book, *Media Unlimited: How the Torrent of Images and Sounds Overwhelms Our Lives*, author Todd Gitlin tells us that a recent A.C. Nielsen survey found that of forty-three nations, the United States ranked third in viewing hours.

Gitlin also found research that showed in 1990, television consumed over 40 percent of the average American's free time. Gitlin found some other interesting facts; for example, the average American child lives in a household with the following:

+ 2.9 televisions

+ 1.8 VCRs

+ 3.1 radios

+ 2.6 tape players

+ 2.1 CD players

+ 1.4 video game players

+ And only 1 computer

These are important facts to remember when you start planning to use broadcast media. It helps you to determine which type of broadcast media you can utilize more effectively. Is your audience listening to the radio? Which stations and why? Are they watching local television programming, national programming, or cable? Why?

THE T-CONNECTOR FORMULA TO THE RESCUE... AGAIN

If you apply the T-Connector Formula to your company's desire to use broadcast media, you will be better able to control the outcome. What are the topics that interest your audience that fit what television viewers want to see? Are these topics the latest news or last week's news?

Should you use local programming, or is your audience living across the nation or across the world? Do they watch *Good Morning America* every day? Does your audience like to watch the *Today Show* instead of *Good Morning America?* Is your audience even available during the times those shows air?

Maybe your audience likes radio better. Topic, timing, and type of media are the vitals you need to determine before approaching broadcast outlets.

CHAPTER FIFTEEN

YOUR AUDIENCE'S CHOICE OF MEDIA

*"Kids could see the mountains of french fries, moms could escape from
meal planning, and dads could escape the hassles of business."*
A quote from Keith Reinhard in John F. Love's book
McDonald's Behind the Arches

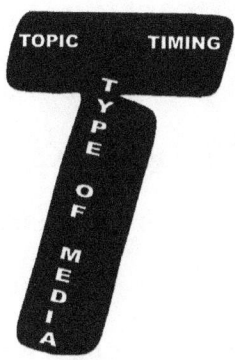

I really do love *The New York Times*. Actually, I'm addicted to that

newspaper. I would love to be printed in that newspaper, but my clients'

audiences do not read *The New York Times*, so my chances of getting a

release printed there are virtually zero.

The top five newspapers in this country are *The Wall Street*

Journal, The New York Times, The Washington Post, USA Today, and *The*

Los Angeles Times. I consult with nonprofit organizations in a small mid-

Ohio community that would rate their readership of these newspapers

as follows:

USA Today	Every now and then
The Wall Street Journal	Every now and then

The New York Times	Seldom
The Washington Post	Even less seldom
The Los Angeles Times	Is there such a paper?

I don't even attempt to send to these newspapers because the people my clients need to reach just do not read this group.

YOU KNOW THE AUDIENCE...YOU HAVE FIT THE TOPIC...YOU KNOW WHEN TO REACH THEM... NOW LET'S GET THE "HOW TO REACH THEM"

One of the strengths of integrated marketing at McDonald's is that the executives at McDonald's continually plan their marketing to reach their audiences. Their marketing research determined they had several target audiences: children, mothers, and fathers.

The company has used mainly television advertising but they have effectively mixed their broadcast media with other media types.

They have also had public relations campaigns for community-based events and for the Ronald McDonald House organization. McDonald's know their audience, how to reach them, and what interests them.

Kids want cool food; moms want quick and easy food; dads want convenient and low-cost food. McDonald's addressed each with a media mix in topic, timing, and type of media.

RESEARCH SHOWS...

What does your research say about your audiences? Do they listen to radio or watch television? What do they read: local or national newspapers, consumer or trade magazines? Or, are they all wired and use the net to get their news and information?

Survey says... Ask your audiences, and they will tell you. Then ask your media for their demographics. Match the two and you have your perfect type of media. This process is not difficult (that is, until you try to reach an international or an ethnic audience).

If you serve a large Hispanic audience, they may be watching English or Spanish television. They may be reading local newspapers or a Spanish-written publication. Or, even to make things even more complicated, your company may serve several ethnic groups. Regardless of who they are, coming from different countries will make for very distinctively different audiences with very different topic and media preferences.

You best plan is to ask each audience what they prefer. Then cater to that preference.

GENERAL MEDIA FACTS

Some interesting facts that can help you determine your audience's type of media include:

+ More women watch television than men.

- More men listen to the radio.

- Midday is the most common time to get the news.

- NBC was reported in *USA Today's* January 6, 2004, issue as the most "upscale" network.

The highest percentage of viewers watching NBC in 2004 earn an annual household income of $75,000 or more. This may not be true today of this particular network, which proves how closely you have to monitor the media.

FIND THE SECOND, THIRD, AND FOURTH CHOICES

Find your audience's first, second, third, and fourth choices for type of media and use a good mix. Never count on one resource. Consumers are fickle and can change their preference for any and many reasons. I love *The New York Times* but there are days at a time that I am too busy to even read the front page.

I use daily local newspapers the most for my news, then *The New York Times*, then the Internet; I click between all three major network morning news programs. I very seldom watch the evening news. My radio is tuned to one classical music station and the three major cities around me, plus one local station.

I am continually changing stations, depending on what I want to hear or need to hear for business-related reasons. I prefer to listen to classical music all day, but I know that I need to monitor my environment for other local, state, and national happenings. In other words, although I have my first preference, I can be reached through multiple types of media at different times of the day.

I can guarantee that my preferences and activities are the norm, not the exception. This means that your audiences can probably be reached via multiple media and multiple choices within each media category. Be prepared with good planning and by using the T-Connector to narrow in on all of the pertinent options.

CHAPTER SIXTEEN

TYPE OF MEDIA AND THE SAMPLE COMPANIES

"Never confuse motion with action."
Ben Franklin

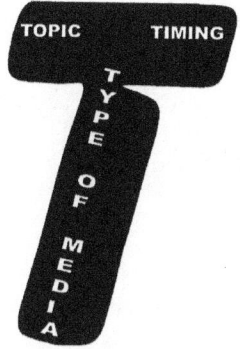

We've looked at topics and timing for press releases and PSAs for both of the sample companies. This section will revisit Chapters Seven and Nine so that we can apply the complete T-Connector Formula and put it into action.

TYPE OF MEDIA: THE TREE TOP COMPANY

This company uses public relations, marketing, advertising, and an integrated communications plan. As such they use newspapers, magazines (both consumer and trade magazines), radio, television, billboards, and direct mail, and their company name and phone number is printed on all of their vehicles.

For just one example of type of media for public relations, let's look back at the free holiday seminar the company is offering. The seminar news was presented in Chapter Seven as a press release for print publications and as a public service announcement for broadcast. In Chapter Nine, timing for the press release and the PSA was discussed.

It was determined that the release needed to be sent to the monthly publications four to five weeks before the event date and two to thee weeks in advance of the event date for the weekly and daily publications. The PSA can be sent several days to one week in advance of the event date.

The targeted audience would include senior citizens, avid gardeners, new residents, garden clubs, and horticulture classes. Remember, females are the decision-makers. A media list for this event would include the following:

- Local daily newspapers.
- Monthly and weekly publications that would reach persons in the area that would have an interest in such an event.
- Radio for the PSA (again, send only to those stations that would have listeners that are interested in the seminar's topic).
- Direct mail to those customers that have purchased new trees in the past or that are listed as new homeowners.
- A flyer to hand out at the sales counters seven to ten days in advance would also help promote the event.
- Since Tree Top uses advertising as a part of their integrated

communications plan, a small ad in the local newspaper would also be part of the promotion plan for this free seminar.

The company has a detailed topic and message, the public relations and marketing department knows when they need to start the promotional efforts, and now they have a list of media types to target.

To effectively promote for the anniversary open house, the media list includes:

+ Newspapers (local, regional, monthlies, weeklies, and dailies).

+ Trade and regional magazines.

+ Radio.

+ Local cable and regional cable television would also be appropriate.

+ Posters, brochures, special imprinted giveaways, and coupons would all help to promote the event and ensure a twenty-first year of business.

TYPE OF MEDIA: COMMUNITY EDUCATIONAL SERVICES

This company is funded through grants, and as such they only have a small amount of advertising money allotted to them by the grant. They can make the advertising budget stretch by buying advertising in the local high school sports programs, in local monthly and weekly publications, and on local cable television programming; all of these are types of media that will reach their audiences.

Being a nonprofit, they can get free airtime on local radio and local cable television programming. The organization does print brochures, flyers, and posters for distribution around the area. The bulk of their promotion, which is planned and implemented through an integrated communications plan, is completed through the effective use of public relations and limited advertising.

One of the most effective promotional venues used by Community Educational Services is that they attend all of the area job fairs, and they host their own educational event two times a year. These are perfect times and places to distribute special event flyers.

Following the topic and timing mentioned in earlier chapters, the media type list for this company to promote their new Web site is as follows:

+ The press release created in Chapter Eight will be sent to all local monthly, weekly, and daily publications as well as all the high school newsletters, college and technical school newsletters, and trade publications, and to a select list of regional newspapers (those within the tricounty area they serve).

+ The PSA detailed in Chapter Eight will be sent to local AM and FM radio and cable television stations.

+ As mentioned, Community Educational Services does have monies in their budget for flyers and posters. They will use some of this budget to print flyers and posters to promote the Web site.

+ They will also ask other Web sites to put a link to their new site and will offer to do the same for those who do include the link.

+ All of their consultants will be encouraged to tell everyone they are working with, including clients and other agencies, about the Web site. There will be an ample supply of flyers available to all customers to distribute.

KEEP IT FRESH, NEW, AND ALWAYS SIMPLE

Varying the type of media helps to get your topic and message spread, but it also helps to keep it new and fresh. Mary Civiello developed the V style to keep communications fresh, she wrote, ""V" is for…Visual, Vocal and Verbal."

Always keep your mind open and your eyes alert to new types of media and new ways to inform and persuade your audience to take your call to action.

While looking for ideas to convince eighteen- to twenty-five-year-old males to come back for more educational assessment testing, the adult education department that I was working for purchased cardboard cell phones that had a telephone ring when the mouthpiece was opened.

The cell phone was mailed in a regular letter-sized envelope. The promotional item had "Call me, I have important information for you" imprinted on the piece. We put the adult education counselor's business card in the die-cut card slot. We had a 60percent return rate using this promotion.

Traditionally, a two to three percent return is thought of as a really good promotion. It was somewhat untraditional but it was the perfect piece to get the attention of eighteen- to twenty-five-year-old males during the year 2002.

CHAPTER SEVENTEEN

SO LET'S MAKE THE CONNECTION

"If you want to convince, speak of interest, not of reason."
Ben Franklin

The focus of marketing and public relations is to get your company or organization's communications read and heard by your publics. The challenge is, how do you make your news get noticed over the hundreds of other news or press releases?

To get your press printed or broadcast, you have to have certain elements built into every message or communication. The T-Connector formula—topic, timing, and type of media— can help you test your news releases to make sure they all have the elements of importance.

PRACTICAL USES FOR THE T-CONNECTOR FORMULA

This section looks at a few successful examples of integrated communications campaigns and applies a few to the formula. After you have determined who you are talking to and what you will be saying to them, you need to determine how to deliver the message; that's when you start applying the T-Connector Formula. Remember some of the questions from previous chapters, and keep asking yourself:

1. Will your audience most likely hear the message on the radio, see it on television, or read it in the newspaper?

2. Does the majority of your publics read the daily local newspaper for their news, or do they read the regional or national papers?

3. Do your target audiences read only trade publications?

4. Would a direct mail campaign reach the greatest number of people? And, does your target audience react to direct mail?

5. Would a billboard work better to reach a more general audience, or are you trying to build an image or name recognition that would fit a billboard?

6. Are your publics more technology oriented, and are they more easily reached through Web sites or email?

7. More than likely, you will need to use multiple types of media to get the message out; if so, which media types would be the most effective for the money?

8. What is the timing of the media: immediate or a few weeks in the future?

9. When is the deadline for the media type?

10. Is your message written for any specific type of media, and can it be adjusted to fit any other type of media?

If your audience is reading and listening and surfing different media, then you have to repeat the message, in a modified form, across all media used.

Remember, the topic and timing has to fit the media. The format also has to match the media type.

A national campaign about orthopedic medicine would be a macro campaign. To get involved in the promo on a micro level, you could easily use the T-Connector with this example to promote a healthcare facility. Basing your news on the big news in your industry, you would need to build your organization's press around this topic, during the same time frame as the national news.

GOT MILK?

The "Got Milk?" public relations campaign is another great example of tying into a national campaign. This campaign used national print and television broadcasts to promote the benefits of drinking milk. This was a perfect example of how a public relations communications plan crossed over into the marketing plan and helped halt the decline in milk sales.

Biggs, California, was considering changing the name of their town (where the Got Milk? campaign began) to Got Milk? The town would have received many benefits such as new computers for all of the schools and a Got Milk Museum. Although the town's residents, in the end, turned down the offer, the Got Milk campaign helped make the town famous.

FOLLOW THE ARCHES

McDonald's fast-food restaurants are the perfect example of using the T-Connector Formula with a media mix.

McDonald's has long been recognized as one of the top marketing and promotion enigmas. Their advertising experts determined that the company had three different target markets:

1. Kids

2. Parents

3. Young adults

After conducting consumer research, the advertising firm found one common perception among McDonald's consumers: McDonald's was not a typical dining out experience, it was also a fun place for families to go.

They (McDonald's) offered something for everyone in the family: action toys and finger foods for the kids, good food and low prices for the parents, and a clean and convenient place to eat. McDonald's develops messages for each of their three audiences (topic). Then they use television as the major media type. And, they develop commercials on a seasonal (timing) basis.

EBAY SUCCESS

The now-famous auction site that was started by two collectors (and which is now one of the most successful dot-com sites) also uses multiple media outlets, which can be fit into the T-Connector Formula.

Most of the company's advertising has been Internet based (type of media). What's really made the company top in its category has been word of mouth (yet another type of media) and the public relations engine.

Because of the company's success, it has had numerous profiles written up in the major business newspapers and magazines, often with major headlines. For example, eBay made the news in 1999 when a human kidney was put up for auction. That same year, 500 pounds of marijuana was listed for auction; eBay again made the news. Some of the headlines were not all that gracious, but the company turned the bad big news of the day into good big news by responding responsibly to the public (which also made the news).

By the time the good big news hit, the company's business had increased, primarily due to those who wanted to gawk at the scene of illegal activity.

eBay has also created an entire community of loyal buyers and sellers through good service, open communications, and acting responsibly with all business transactions.

When you apply this to the T-Connector Formula, it looks like the following:

+ Topic=controversy, bad news, good news, community based

+ Timing=responding appropriately to the bad news and

creating good news from bad

- Type of media= Internet, word of mouth, print and broadcast news

HITS THE TARGET

Another prime example of how a major corporation uses integrated communications plans and how the T-Connector Formula applies is Target, the hip and stylish department store chain.

Target stores nationwide make local and national news by donating a percentage of their profits back to their communities. Plus, the company makes public relations news by hiring famous clothing designers to develop products for their stores. Because of some of their lines of merchandise, they have been tagged as "Cheap Chic," and they have created a number of public relations messages using a variety of media types.

Make no mistake: The company does use a lot of advertising as part of their marketing and communications plans, but they have derived much newsprint space with their public relations news.

HP'S TAKEOVER MARKETING CAMPAIGN

In November of 2002, the newly merged HP (Hewlett-Packard acquired Compaq Computer in May 2002) started a new advertising campaign that was designed to last over several years and was predicted to cost several hundred million dollars. The campaign was set up to show that HP is a company with depth and ready and able to tackle any computing challenge.

The campaign included print ads, television promotions, online advertising, and billboards. With the main message "+hp=everything is possible," the company used multiple types of media to deliver the message. Print ads were purchased for major newspapers such as *The New York Times* and *The Wall Street Journal* and for national business magazines such as *Time*, *BusinessWeek*, and *Newsweek*.

Paid advertising used the same message as the public relations messages.

USING CONFLICT AND CONTROVERSY

There are times that controversy can be used for the betterment of an organization. eBay used controversy to build trust with their publics. Caller ID is another example of a good controversy; caller ID showed how topic and timing could be combined to the company's advantage. By now we all know that with caller ID you can see the phone number displayed on your telephone, and you can answer if you want or you can ignore the call. When this service was first offered, the issue or big news of the time was whether the service violated the caller's privacy. Believe it or not, the controversy actually helped sell the service.

How about wearing a seat belt in your car? There was a time when automobile drivers and passengers did not have to wear seat belts.

Safety awareness resulted from an extensive public relations campaign promoting "Buckle Up."

It started in the 1980s by the United States automotive industry. It was promoted entirely through public relations efforts. The automotive industry used interactive displays, celebrity endorsements, letter writing campaigns, and several widely publicized public relations events.

The controversy was a debate that wearing a seat belt would prohibit the exit of the car if the driver were to plunge into a body of water and sink. Such controversy allowed the supporters and nay-sayers to openly discuss the pros and cons, which in turn provided more and more press. Did it work? According to statistics at safetycenter.navy.mil/ashore/MotorVehicle/clickit/nationalstatistics.htm the number of people buckling up rose to 79 percent in 2003 from 58 percent in 1994.

MAKING THE CONNECTION

There are just so many ways to make connections these days. Look at the wave of interest created by Youtube and Facebook and other similar sites on the Internet. If nothing else, these sites have created entire communities societies that have as many similarities as they do differences.

You may not use these sites yourself, or maybe you do. Regardless of your own personal opinion or usage of the sites, if you can reach your company's audience there, then there you must go.

If you continue to let the T-Connector Formula help you develop and deliver, you'll make the connection where and when you need to.

CHAPTER EIGHTEEN

MAKING THE CONNECTION
WITH THE SAMPLE COMPANIES

"Get experience any way you can."
#17 of 100 Secrets of Successful People

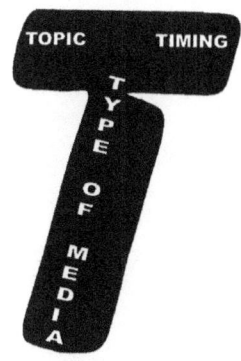

After coming this far with this book, you should now have a good sense of what marketing, public relations, and integrated communications planning is all about. If you are thinking promotion, promotion, promotion, you have been paying close attention to what has been printed in these pages, and you can give yourself an A. If you also included using the T-Connector Formula to achieve promotion, promotion, promotion, you get an A+ and will reap much press time and space.

THE SAMPLE COMPANIES HAVE SHOWN US THE WAY

Earlier chapters gave you examples of how each sample company would use topic, timing, and type of media as individual parts of the T-Connector Formula. Each chapter touched on using the formula as a complete recipe for promotional success. This section takes the connection one step further by applying more theory to practical everyday uses.

THE TREE TOP COMPANY PREPARES ITS PROMOTIONAL PLAN

This book has talked about marketing, public relations, communications plans, and promotion, promotion, promotion. All of these concepts, practices, theory, disciplines, or whatever term you want to assign to them are really about getting your company's news, views, and information to the public. For the Tree Top Company, they call their integrated communications planning a promotional plan.

They use checklists of questions that get assigned to every project, large scale and small, to ensure they get the topic, the timing, and the right type of media in place to reach their targeted audience or public.

The only thing worse than not getting anyone to hear your message is for people who have absolutely no interest whatsoever to hear your message. If the topic is sent to the wrong people at the wrong time using inappropriate channels, the message gets trashed. If you send a message meant for persons over fifty-five years of age to someone that might have turned a sensitive forty-five, you will undoubtedly anger that youngling.

This would be worst than no press because that forty-five-year-old is going to tell twenty of his or her friends what an insult you sent them.

When the promotional plan for the free holiday seminar was developed, the marketing and public relations professionals met to discuss the planning for the seminar, and they started by asking the following questions:

1. What are the topic and the tone of the message that would most effectively reach the identified target audience for this seminar? (topic)

2. Is this message informative, persuasive, or both? (for the seminar, the message would be both)

3. Where is the audience for this seminar getting their other news and information? (type of media)

4. Does this audience read the newspaper, watch the television, or surf the Web site for their daily news? (type of media)

5. Is this a good topic for print and broadcast? (topic)

6. Do we need to tailor the message to each type of media or does one message fit all? Will we have more than one way to get this topic published? (topic)

7. When do we have to get the releases, PSAs, posters, brochures, and all other promotional materials used for this seminar to the various types of media? (timing)

8. Is this a seasonally related topic? (topic and timing)

9. What are the deadlines? (timing)

As the company went through their promotional planning for the seminar, they asked and answered all of the above questions while quietly applying the T-Connector Formula. The plan they developed has been detailed for you in Chapters Seven, Nine, and Eleven.

COMMUNITY EDUCATIONAL SERVICES

Community Educational Services' promotional plan for the launch of their new Web site would ask the same questions but would be answered much differently than those at the Tree Top Company. Nonetheless, the organization starts by asking the questions, developing the answers, and setting up an appropriate promotional plan. One difference is that the message strategy for the launch of the Web site is more on the informative side versus informative/persuasive for Tree Top's seminar.

Applying the T-Connector Formula helps in making the media connection and ensures that all aspects of the promotional or communications plan is considered. Do we have a topic that is newsworthy? Do we have an audience defined that would be interested in the topic? Is the topic seasonal or related to the big news of the time? What are the message strategies we need to use to get the message received properly?

Community Educational Services needed to answer timing questions, such as when are the deadlines for each of the media types we will send to? Is the topic related to a particular time of the year or to the big news of the day? The launch of the Web site is related to the big news because of the increased everyday reliance upon computer technology. It could also be themed to back school or prepare your graduating senior for fall entry into college.

THE T-CONNECTOR FORMULA CONNECTION

Both sample companies have lots of activities and events happening throughout their year that are newsworthy. Both companies can set up a yearlong media calendar and develop media lists that will help to get their news to their publics. As detailed in Chapter Eleven, both companies use a mix of media types and do not rely on one type in particular.

There are many companies, for example, McDonald's that use more television than any other type of media. The company determined, through much market research, that television is the best way to reach their audiences. McDonald's does modify the topic and the timing for seasonal promotions. They also apply timing to when during the day to televise their commercials.

You don't see many commercials for McDonald's during the late-night television shows such as David Letterman or Conan O'Brien. Why? If you were to call and ask the market research department or the marketing department at McDonald's, their most likely answer would be because their target audiences are not watching television at that time of the night.

When you start using the T-Connector Formula, you will actively pursue the topic, timing, and type of media questions and answers. After using it successfully for a short time, the formula will become second nature and you will apply each component and each question and answer automatically.

The media have very defined processes that they like to see followed by everyone submitting news. Some of their rules may seem cumbersome and even unfair. Keep in mind that editors of both print and broadcast media types are overwhelmingly busy and although they operate under a set of standards, they openly express these standards to anyone who cares to ask.

Find out what makes the media on your media list happy, ask questions, apply the T-Connector Formula, and enjoy the printed fruits of your labor.

CHAPTER NINETEEN

KEEPING THE CONNECTION

"Think of these things whence you come,
where you are going and to whom you must account."
Ben Franklin

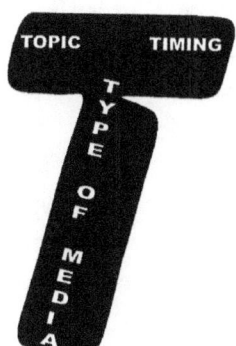

You've tried the T-Connector Formula and it worked. You made a media connection. Your company got great coverage in one of the top trade magazines in the industry.

Don't stop now. Keep your media connections and grow them.

Nourishing your media connections includes using the T-Connector

Formula to do the following:

TOPIC

+ Be creative. Be open-minded to new media outlets.

+ Find your company's news in all the big news.

+ Keep in mind that when you call a reporter on the phone to pitch a story, you only have a few minutes to pique their interest. Always identify yourself; ask if it is a good time to talk or when would be a good time for YOU to call back; let the reporter know you know who they are and what they write or broadcast. Take about thirty to sixty seconds, no more than about two or three lines, and explain the idea and why their readers or listeners will be interested. Always ask if the reporter if he or she is interested!

+ Target the right journalists who want your news. Vocus.com published survey results in April 2002 that suggested that over 70percent of the Vocus survey respondents (journalists and reporters) wanted companies to pitch news only to the reporters that would be interested in their topics.

+ One of the most important keys to successful media relations can be found in your relationship with reporters. To build that relationship and keep it strong, you become a resource for news instead of a distraction. Send or call them with pertinent, applicable news.

+ Send reporters only the newsworthy information generated by your company.

+ Always find the local angle in your news reporting.

TIMING

+ Be mindful of the tough job and the do-or-die deadlines that the media work with, day in and day out.

+ Make releases relate to the time of the year, make the news relevant to the reader.

+ Send releases in plenty of time for publication or coverage.

If you get your information to the media days or hours before an event or a new product announcement, forget about getting good coverage. Politicians and government-related events may be able to get spur-of-the-moment coverage, but the average small to medium-sized company or organization will only get such coverage for bad news.

To get the good news into the hands and heads of your publics, the timing has to be planned to fit the time of the year and you have to get it to the media before their deadlines.

TYPE OF MEDIA

+ Update your media lists with up-to-date contact information on a yearly basis.

+ Add new media outlets to the list as you find them.
+ Watch, listen, and read the local, regional, and national news for topics and timing relating to your organization.

+ Use the Internet to monitor changes in media.

+ Read available publications that offer insight into media relations, media's use of technology, and trends in topics that the media are interested in covering.

+ Monitor your company's competition to keep track of their media connections.

+ Keep in touch with your company's target audiences to see where they are getting their daily news. Survey, call them, talk with them, and ask where they get their consumer news and information.

+ Use the media outlets your audiences recommend.

THINK LIKE A REPORTER

Put yourself in the reporter's shoes, at their keyboard, think like they think, and process the news like they process the interests of their readers and editors. Once you establish connections with the reporters in your area, continue to talk to them, ask them what they are interested in, read or listen to their news presentations, know them, and let them know you.

Your public relations goal is to position your news pitches for more placements, better and bigger placements. The goal of every reporter, be they news or broadcast, is to obtain more space or more time. The two professions complement each other when both sides are working for the common good of the reader or listener.

IT'S NOT OVER WITH THE COVERAGE…FOLLOW-UP, FOLLOW-UP, FOLLOW-UP

When you do get good coverage, especially from a local reporter, it is always a great idea to call, email, or send a quick thank-you note. However you do it, make sure to thank the reporter for the effort and for the good coverage. There is no question you will do so with sincerity because we all appreciate good press.

You can also let the reporter know how effective the feature was. Did the article increase student registration? Did you get a full house at a free lecture because of an interview with a local cable talk show? Did an article create better awareness and understanding from the community? Let the reporter know just what the article meant to your organization and to the public you are trying to reach.

CHAPTER TWENTY

CROSSING THE T-CONNECTION

*"I freely confess that what success I have had in my family
be attributed more to the public press than to nearly all other causes."*
P.T. Barnum

There has to be a section mentioning the mechanics of how to contact the media and a list of resources you can refer to in efforts to make your communications more effective. This is it.

CAN'T LIVE WITH THEM, CAN'T LIVE WITHOUT THEM

Media and public relations people need each other more than either will admit. You can find all kinds of comments made by public relations people about the media and all kinds of unkind remarks from the media about public relations people. Both professions have specific jobs to do, which involve getting news to the public.

On slow news days, the media are hoping for public relations people to call. On heavy news days, the media are bothered by public relations calls for coverage.

THE MECHANICS OF CONTACTING THE MEDIA

101PublicRelations.com offers *52 Tips for Kick-Butt News Releases (and Bonehead Mistakes to Avoid)* along with the seven deadly sins to avoid when contacting the media. The recommendations include suggestions such as making sure you provide information that is complete, accurate, and specific and no longer than two pages in length.

Avoid sending releases too late or sending release with little or no news value but that instead contain blatant commercialism. Don't forget your contact name and phone number, and never call after sending a release to find out if the reporter got the release.

This is all good advice. Press releases that are over two pages long take too long to read. If the topic is interesting and the reporter decides to look into covering it and cannot find the contact person or phone number to call, the release will be forgotten. Include just the facts, packed with the reasons why the readers will care. No fluffy words or hidden commercialism. Leave your superlatives at home to use for that romance or sci-fi novel you are writing.

It is a terrible idea to call and ask if someone in the newsroom received your press release. Every media outlet is receiving more releases than they can keep track of or print. If you add to their workload by calling, you can be assured that they will decide not to cover your topic.

If you are pitching an exclusive idea, go ahead and follow up with a phone call or an email, if acceptable. Calling about a feature is OK but calling about a news release is never acceptable.

NEW WAVES...NEW RESOURCES

Technology continues to shape our lives. In the public relations and marketing business, effects are felt stronger every day. The New Age young adults entering the workforce read their news from a different source than the readers of the past.

We don't just channel surf the television waves or scan the radio waves, we also surf the net. News is coming at us 24/7 from every corner of the world. The United States consumer market makes news every hour. The Monday through Friday, 9 to 5 workforce or lifestyle no longer exists. There isn't any rest on Sundays.

It is hard to keep up, and it is even harder to compete. So how do you make it to the top of the media pile without being the central figure in a car chase through California or by selling malfunctioning tires that cause vehicles to overturn?

Promotions and communications have to be adaptable, acceptable, and communicable. Keep up with the times, know thy audiences, and change with the times. Keep your eyes peeled, keep your ears open, and be on the lookout for new media resources. Track the trends of how your audience is receiving their news. Stay on top media lists by keeping constant contact with those media resources.

Read the publications and the reporters in your area: nationally, regionally, and internationally. There may be reporters you really don't want to catch the attention of; you don't want to hide from them— because you can't—you just may not want to invite them into your company or organization.

The only way to know who and where and when to call the reporter that has an interest in your company's news is to read, watch, talk to, and listen to the media. If the latest news resource is Internet based, guess where you should spend time getting your own news? At the newest, hippest dot.com that is delivering today.

An example is www.nakednews.com. Hundreds or thousands of people are still logging on to this site just to see the news anchors strip while reading the day's national news headlines. Is it considered a serious news resource?

The site got mentioned and featured a number of the national networks' morning shows. Is it a news resource that the average news hound is monitoring? Better check it out before making that decision.

LIST OF RESOURCES TO HELP YOU FIND YOUR MEDIA RESOURCES

How can you keep up with it all? Do what you do best. Monitor your environments. Work with your instincts. Communicate with your audience(s) the way they want. The following lists may help you keep up-to-date with the latest and the greatest news and media resources.

WEB SITES
www.radio-locator.com
www.acp.com
101publicrelations.com
www.yahoo.com
www.lycos.com
www.google.com
www.naa.org/presstime
www.publicityhound.com
www.mediatoolcase.com
www.bernsteincom.com
www.newspaperlink.com
www.naa.org (Newspaper Association of America)
www.napsinfo.com

BOOKS
Writer's Market
Bacon's Media Directory
International Directory of Little Magazines & Small Presses

MEDIA MAGAZINES
Adweek
Advertising Age
American Demographics Magazine
Journalism & Mass Communication Quarterly
Mediaweek
Media Life
Presstime
PRWeek
The Daily Planet
The Write News
Writer's Digest

MEDIA RELATIONS NEWSLETTERS

Partyline	www.partylinepublishing.com
Infocom	www.infocomgroup.com
Media Relations Report	www.ragan.com
ProfNet	www.profnet.com

CHAPTER TWENTY-ONE

KEEPING T-CONNECTED TO YOUR AUDIENCE

"There is an ancient proverb: 'Men resemble the times more than they do their fathers.'"
J. Walker Smith and Ann Clurman

Rocking the Ages

While the T-Connector Formula is ageless, the answers produced by the formula will continually change. A positive side effect of the using the formula is that it will make you review your audiences' needs automatically. But, remember the success of using the formula does not allow for any assumptions. The old computer term GIGO (Garbage In, Garbage Out) applies to the T-Connector Formula and the results you get from the data you feed it.

KEEP IN TOUCH ...KEEP CONNECTED

Consumers are a fickle bunch. They change on a whim and turn on a dime. Generations change. Demographics change. I once attended a seminar where the "get to know you" opening activity had a room full of female educators divided into groups by the kind of car each woman drove.

The highest number of women in attendance were thirty-something teachers who had more than one child. That particular group all drove minivans. The twenty-something's group drove SUVs, while the forty-something's that all had grown children drove four-door sedans.

Many of the forty-something's said they had sold their minivans years ago. As these women changed age groups, they changed driving preferences. Along with that change, they also had a change in their food tastes and restaurants, they experienced a change in their reading tastes and habits, and their spending habits changed as well.

Later in that same icebreaker session, we ended up in groups according to our favorite types of vacation locations. Those with young children preferred the Disney Worlds and the Cedar Points, while those with empty nests favored the beaches and the big cities. It is a must that you read, watch, and listen to what is happening in the world. Then, drill those events and trends down to what's important to your target audiences.

For example, DVD players have been reported as the fastest-selling consumer electronics item ever sold. Such a tidbit of news should be important to you and your media connections because it could be a strong indicator of what is happening with your audience's spare time. Does this piece of news really matter to your audiences? Be certain and ask them.

HOW OFTEN SHOULD YOU USE THE FORMULA?

Use the T-Connector Formula every time you start on a press release or PSA or consider pitching a television show. The more times you use the T-Connector Formula, the more second nature it will become for you to ask yourself, Does the topic fit? Is the timing right? Is this the right type of media?

Hopefully these questions will lead you to keep in touch with your company's business environment, the latest media preferences, and what your audiences want.

The T-Connector Formula does not promise you a media connection. Nor does it shelter magic beans. The media business is fast paced and driven by egos and the need to be first. First with the news, first in ratings, first in print: They just really like to be first.

If you use the time of those working in media effectively and give them good information in a clear, readable, and understandable format (and if you don't make reporters and newscasters work too hard), your company's news will make will reach your audiences. If you test your news to make

157

sure it fits your audience, they will read it, listen to it, or watch it.

It is hard to believe in this day of celebrity news and sensationalism, but the true power of the media is truth.

APPENDIX A

THE T-CONNECTOR FORMULA

WHAT IS THE T-CONNECTOR FORMULA?

There are three issues that are affected by the T-Connector Formula:

1) Having the right topic

2) At the right time (and before deadline)

3) Directing it to the right type of media to cover it

The T-Connector Formula helps business owners, managers, nonprofit organization directors, and public relations or marketing professionals get the right message to the right type of media in the proper time frame. Put the three of these elements together, as illustrated below, and they make a T-connection. And, more importantly, they can help you get all the right elements in place to make media connections.

Topic Timing
T
y
p
e
o
f
m
e
d
i
a

T-CONNECTOR QUESTIONS FOR
MARKETING AND PUBLIC RELATIONS

Topic: Informative or Persuasive

Who is the audience?
Why does the audience need to know this information?
What does the audience need to know?
Can the topic be themed to the time of the year?
Can the topic be related to the big news of the day?
What is the message strategy for the topic: informative or persuasive?

Timing

When does the audience need to know this information?
Is this an immediate or future message?
What is the time of year that best fits the topic?
Can the message get to the media before their deadline?
What is the big news of the day?
Is there a seasonal theme that can be used at this time?

Type of Media: Informative or Persuasive

Where will the audience most likely read or hear the topic?
Which medium reaches the biggest part of your target audience?
What types of media does the message or topic fit the best?
Can it be modified to fit multiple types of media?

APPENDIX B

FLOWCHARTS OF MARKETING AND PUBLIC RELATIONS PROCESSES

MARKETING PROCESS FLOWCHART

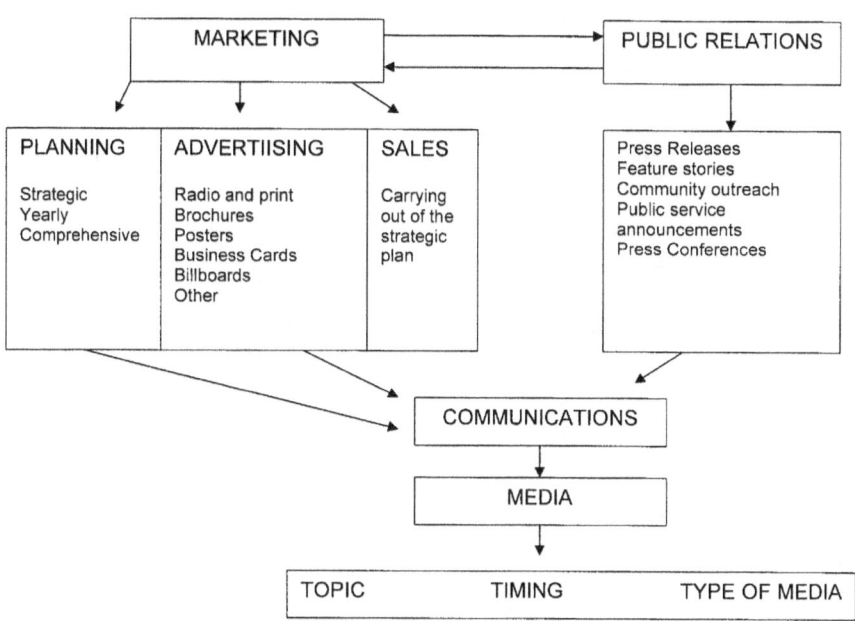

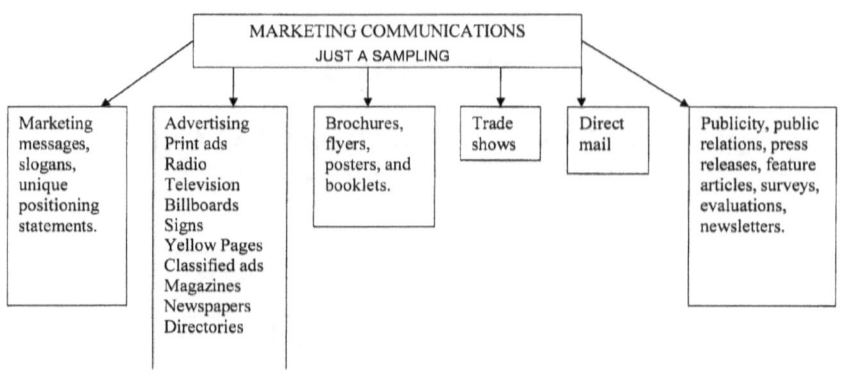

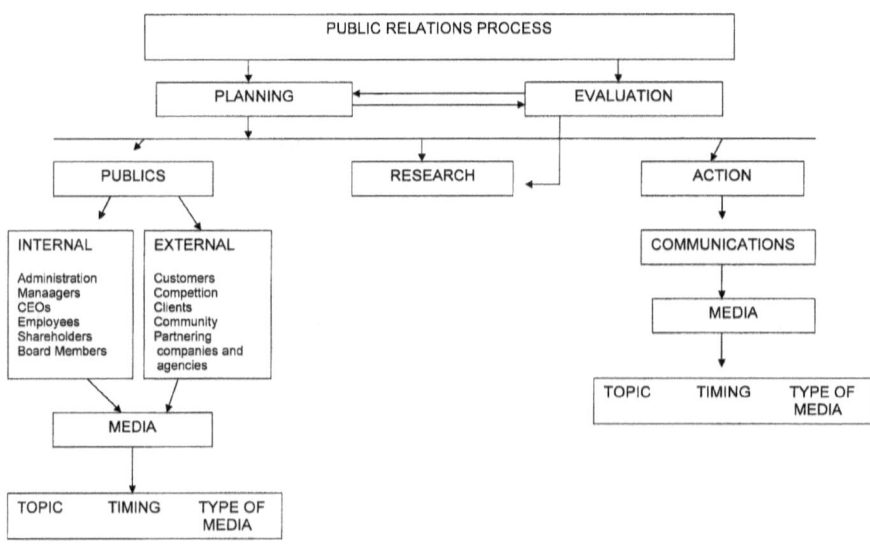

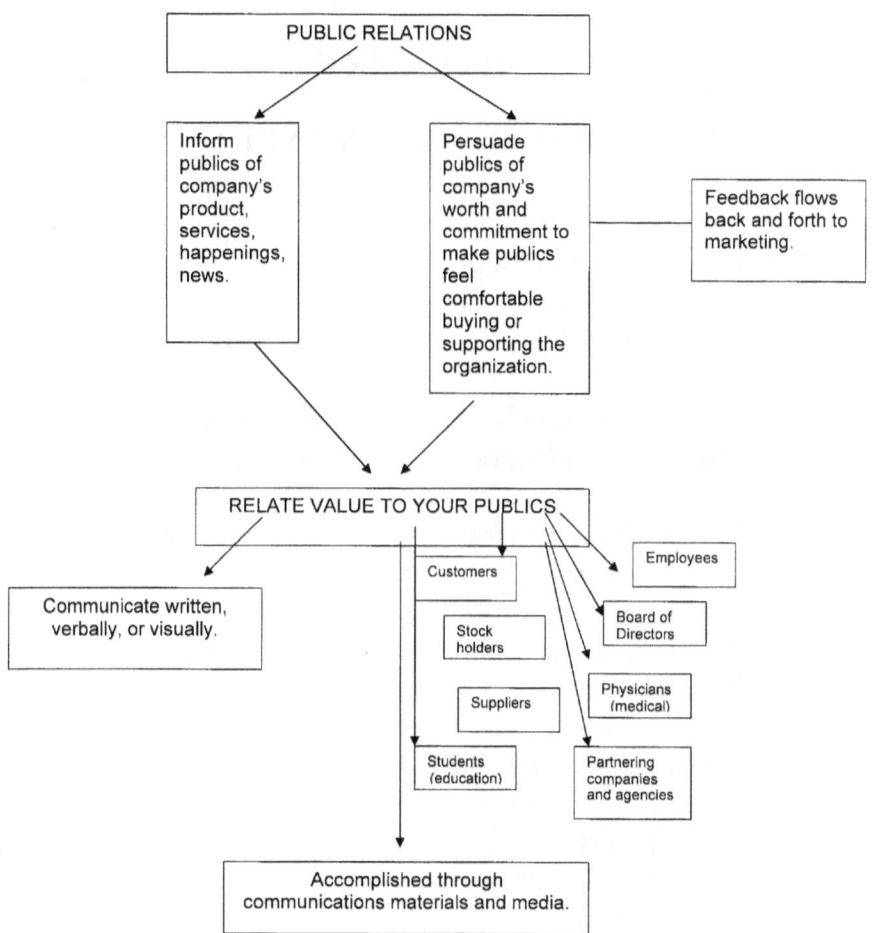

APPENDIX C

SOME INTERESTING MEDIA TYPE STATISTICS

TELEVISION STATISTICS

+ There are over 1,600 licensed television stations.

+ Television is so effective because it combines printed words, spoken words, pictures, sounds, and video.

+ A fifty-eight-second feature on the television news is considered a major storyline.

+ Television still ranks the number one place for Americans to get their daily news.

+ Some of the terms applied to television include:
    o   Sound bites: ten to thirty seconds in length
    o   Fast cuts
    o   Graphically interesting presentations
    o   Line shots

+ The different types of news include broadcast news, network news, and cable news.

+ Community access stations are often looking for programs to air.

+ Some stations adopt a cause.

+ Many stations broadcast a community calendar.

RADIO STATISTICS

There are over 12,000 licensed radio stations in the United States.

Radio is ubiquitous people have their radios on at work, in the care and at home.

Radio is used as a quick source of information in the morning, such as weather, traffic, sports scores, and news.

80 percent of the population listens to a radio daily.

It is a person-to-person medium that's based on and flourishes because of conversation.

The medium is driven by sound bites and the on-air personalities.

Most radio is locally produced with local news, weather, traffic, etc.

Writing for radio uses a different style and format than when writing for print. Radio news releases should be more conversational and immediate. Use fewer words, according to the word chart that follows.

The following word counts can be used to assist your radio writing. Just keep in mind the person reading the copy can have a fast or slow voice, so the word count may not reflect that.

Time	Word Count
10 seconds	25 words
20 seconds	30 words
30 seconds	45–50 words
50 seconds	65–70 words
60 seconds	125–130 words

Use three rules when writing for radio: Write with immediacy, make it brief, and make it relevant.

Typical radio and television contacts:

Type of Submission	Who to Contact
News items	News director
PSAs	Public service director
Public affairs and events	Community calendar editor

INTERNET STATISTICS

The average Web site user has seven online sessions during the week and spends over three hours a week online.

Remember when writing for the Internet to provide links to research or information sites.

Remember to include a search function.

Persons reading their news on the Internet like the news to be immediate, and they like the news to change often, but the news must be accurate.

Make your news a quick read.

Your news or press releases can be put on the Internet in the same format as they are sent to newspapers and magazines.

NEWSPAPER STATISTICS

There are over 1,600 daily newspapers with 62 million in circulation.

There are over 7,000 weekly newspapers and over 5,000 trade publications.

Weeklies and monthlies offer opportunities for regular columns and regular letters to the editor.

Weeklies will many times use photographs.

Two out of three dailies have 25,000 or less in circulation.

Weeklies and monthlies are more socially oriented and provide more local coverage than many of the daily newspapers.

If you just send news releases to the daily newspapers, the maximum circulation is 58 million. If you send your news releases to all of the dailies and weeklies, you can get up to 137 million in circulation.

According to some reports, the newspaper remains the most read news media.

Don't forget community ethnic newspapers.

General newspaper contacts include:

Type of Submission	Who to Contact
News items	News editor or reporter
Human interest	Features editor
Letter to the editor	Editor
Events	Community calendar editor
Purchase ads	Advertising manager or representatives

The top five U.S. daily newspapers by circulation are:

USA Today	2.1 million
The Wall Street Journal	1.8 million
The New York Times	1.2 million
The Los Angeles Times	Over 900,000
The Washington Post	Over 790,000

MAGAZINE STATISTICS

There are over 12,000 periodicals in the United States.

Ben Franklin is credited with originating the concept of a magazine when he published *General Magazine* in 1741.

156.3 million U.S. adults read one or more magazines each month.

Magazines are more targeted to specific readers than newspapers.

Readers will keep a magazine much longer than they will a newspaper.

Magazines get circulated throughout a home, an office, amongst friends.

Uses press releases when the news serves their readers' economic or professional needs.

Reader's Digest reaches over 48 million people each month.

BIBILOGRAPHY

Bivins, T. H. (1999). *Public Relations Writing—The Essentials of Style and Format*. Chicago, Illinois: National Textbook Company.

Brown, Jerry. *Monday Morning Media Minute*. www.pr-impact.com

Burke, Doris. "The True Meaning of Twitter", August 18, 2008. Fortune Magazine, pages 39 – 42.

Burrell, D. and Lueche, R. (2000). *The eBay Phenomenon*. New York: John Wiley & Sons.

Civiello, Mary, (2008). *Communication Counts*. New Jersey: John Wiley & Sons, Inc.

Cutlip, S. M., Center, A. H., & Broom, G. M. (2000). *Effective Public Relations*, Eighth edition. New York: Prentice Hall.

Debelak, Don, (2000). *Streetwise Marketing Plan*. Holbrook, Massachusetts: Adams Media Corporation.

Gitlin, T. (2002). *Media Unlimited: How the Torrent of Images and Sounds Overwhelms Our Lives*. New York: Henry Holt.

Harris, T. L. (1998). *Value-Added Public Relations*. Chicago, Illinois: NTC Business Books.

Hillenbrand, L. (2001). *Seabiscuit: An American Legend*. New York: Ballentine Books.

Humes, J. C. (1995). *Wit & Wisdom of Benjamin Franklin*, New York: Gramercy Books.

Internet Usage Demographics. Cyberatlas.internet.com.

Kalbfeld, B. (2001). *Associated Press Broadcast News Handbook: A Manual of Techniques and Practices.* Dayton, OH: The Associated Press.

Levine, M. (1993). *Guerrilla P.R.* New York: HarperBusiness.

Levine, M, (2008). *Guerrilla P.R. 2.0.* New York: HarperBusiness.

Love, J. F. (1986/1995). *McDonald's Behind the Arches,* Revised edition. New York: Bantam Books.

Niven, D. (2002). *The 100 Simple Secrets of Successful People.* San Francisco: Harper.

"Noteworthy Ideas." (2002). Flyer published by North American Prescis Syndicate.

Ries, A. and Ries, L. (2002). *The Fall of Advertising & The Rise of PR.* New York: Harper Business.

Roberts, Sam, (January 16, 2007). *www.nytimes.com/2007/01/16/us/16census.html?hp&ex=11*

Smith, J. W. and Clurman, A. (1997). *Rocking the Ages: The Yankelovich Report on Generational Marketing.* New York: Harper Collins.

USA Today (January 6, 2004) Lifeline Column, page 1D.

www.incredibleegg.org/about_ads.html

www.gotmilk.com . Brand History

www.managementhelp.org. PR Defined

www.marketingpower.com. *The American Marketing Association Releases New Definition for Marketing.* American Marketing Association press release (January 14, 2008).

www.wikipedia.com/wiki/got_ milk

Yale, David R. with Carothers, Andrew J (2001). *The Publicity Handbook, New Edition.* New York: McGraw Hill.

Zig Ziglar (1984). *Secrets of Closing the Sale.* New Jersey: Fleming H. Revell Company